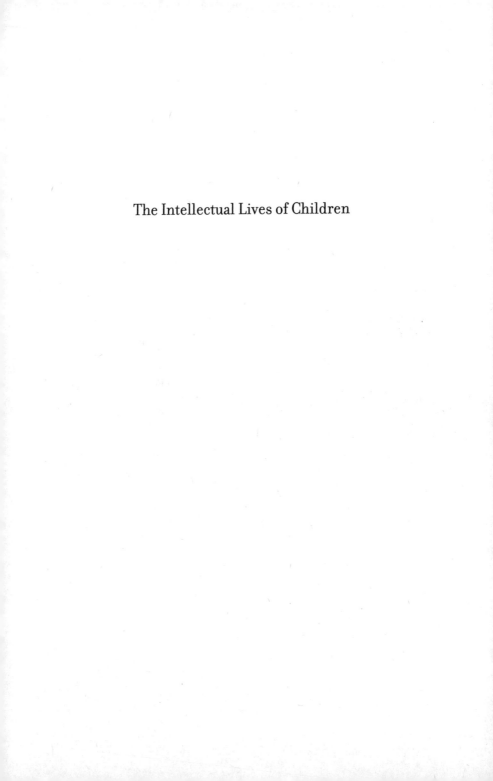

The Intellectual Lives of Children

The
Intellectual
Lives of
Children

Susan Engel

Harvard University Press

Cambridge, Massachusetts
London, England

Printed in the United States of America

First Harvard University Press paperback edition, 2022
First printing

Library of Congress Cataloging-in-Publication Data

Names: Engel, Susan L., 1959– author.
Title: The intellectual lives of children / Susan Engel.
Description: Cambridge, Massachusetts : Harvard University Press, 2021. |
Includes bibliographical references and index.
Identifiers: LCCN 2020022434 | ISBN 9780674988033 (cloth) |
ISBN 9780674278646 (pbk.)
Subjects: LCSH: Cognition in children. | Children—Intellectual life. |
Youth—Intellectual life. | Education. | Age and intelligence.
Classification: LCC BF723.C5 E488 2021 | DDC 155.4/13—dc23
LC record available at https://lccn.loc.gov/2020022434

For Henry and Lina

Contents

The Intellectual Lives of Children

1

Prelude

My mother was easygoing and generous. Some might say cavalier. That must be why she let me know, when I was six, that I could use her charge account at two important stores. The first was the small general store just down the road in the farm town where we lived. I could get there on my bike in four minutes. On my way I passed potato fields, a pig barn, the village green, the cemetery, the farmhouse where my grandmother Helen lived, and finally, the Sagaponack General Store. Luckily for me, the store was also just down the street from the red shingled one-room school house where I attended first grade, and to which I commuted on my bike. You could buy many things at that general store: eggs, milk, bacon, bread, laundry detergent, disposable diapers, bologna, mustard, and potato chips. The store was also home to our post office, and the father and son who ran the place were postmasters as well as store clerks. But all that mattered to me was the penny candy counter, covered by a tall, gracious dome of glass. Standing on your side of the counter you could point to the candy you wanted, and Lee or Merrall Hildreth would reach in from their side to take out the pieces you desired. Lee was old (though not as old as I then thought)—grouchy and impatient. His son, Merrall, was tolerant and sunny and we always hoped he'd be the one to help us make our selections. What a boon it was to me that my school was so close. At lunchtime my friends and I could pedal over, buy some candy, and be back in no time, ready for the afternoon of lessons to begin. But I was the luckiest, it seems. Other children would bring their quarters and dimes—which could buy you a lot of Cow Tails, red shoelaces, Tootsie Rolls, and Heath bars (my particular favorites)—but I could simply ask Merrall or Lee to write it down on my parents' account. I didn't buy more than the other children, I just flung myself into it with greater absorption. I was as thrilled to file away all the details of different candy types as I was to eat them. I still have an encyclopedic knowledge of sweets.

But that wasn't the only place my mother allowed me to procure what I craved. The other store was even more fabulous, though somewhat less accessible. It was Keene's bookstore, in the large and busy town of Southampton, a twenty-minute drive from my home. Between the ages of seven and fourteen, I often visited friends in Southampton on Saturdays. My mother would drop me off for a few hours of adventure. The girl I most often met up with was Michele Vahradian. Her parents owned the Southampton dry cleaner's, so she was already in town when I arrived. Her mother would give her ten dollars, which seemed wonderfully extravagant to me. She'd buy tiny glass animal figures, and we'd go to the luncheonette, Sip 'n Soda, and order lime rickeys and hamburgers. Often Michele would pay for my lunch because I was on a tighter leash. My mother would give me three dollars, which didn't quite cover the tchotchkes and snacks that we liked. After Sip 'n Soda, we'd head down the block to Keene's, where I could lose myself. As I remember him, Mr. Keene had pitted, pouchy, red skin, coarse white hair that lay across his scalp like an old sweater, an ungainly hobble, and a gravelly voice. I'm pretty sure he smoked in the store, which was allowed in those days. As well as being a book-lover he was known for his irascibility—but not by me. He must have been amused by my love of his store. I'd come in with an expectation of guilty pleasures, like some people must feel entering a porn shop. I'd head straight for the shelf of children's fiction—*Nancy Drew, The Borrowers, A Little Princess,* and on one bonanza of a day, the complete *Chronicles of Narnia.* He'd usually leave me to find my own selection, and then, as if I were a grown-up customer, graciously take the particular book from my hands, write down the title, author, and cost in his ledger, and add it to my mother's account. I don't ever remember my mother telling me I shouldn't have bought a book, not even when my taste turned to Keene's selection of large, glossy, coffee-table volumes, each about a different movie star. I think they cost about $18.00 each. Even for a family like mine, who took a trip most years and lived in a spacious house, that was a lot to spend.

God, how I lusted for those books. Hedy Lamarr, Marlene Dietrich, Greta Garbo, the all-time love of my nine-year life, Clark Gable—and others, too many to list. But I didn't grab them all up at once. Maybe I knew my mother would draw the line at that. Instead, I'd choose one and yearn for it for a while, looking it over Saturday after Saturday until I was ready (or felt permission) to buy it. Then the process would begin again, until I brought home another one. Mr. Keene must have stocked only a few at a time because months would sometimes go by without a new title to tempt me. I'd wander in with Michele, perfectly content to browse other sections of the store. Then, grouchy, gravel-toned Mr. Keene would come over and say, in what seemed to me a diffident voice, "Susie. I got in something new. Take a look at this." And from one of the many messy and tall piles of books that filled the surfaces and most of the floor space of his store, he'd pull out a volume I'd never seen before—once, it was Marilyn Monroe, another day Rita Hayworth, and another time Gary

Cooper. I'd drool over the new treasure for a while, leafing through it slowly, marveling at the gorgeous black-and-white portraits of my newest Hollywood crush. But that wasn't all those pages offered me. The books were filled with information and stories about where the stars had grown up, what their childhoods had been like, how they had gotten their first roles. I couldn't get enough of all that biographical material. Because I was able to buy so freely, I ended up with a hefty and absorbing collection. I'd return to my pile of books again and again, poring over the text as much as the photos. Often when I went back to them, I'd concentrate on a certain kind of information—sometimes paying attention to their upbringing, other times focusing on their marriages. I recall making a mental list of the places they had all lived. I was organizing the information into various schema, creating a surprisingly dense network of knowledge. At one point I even made a little inventory of the most salacious anecdote associated with each star. I can remember being particularly horrified and riveted by Jean Harlow's abusive first marriage. I'm sure no one realized, as I sprawled on the couch, ran around on the grass outside of our house, or looked after my baby sister, that these matters were so much on my mind.

Few adults think carefully about the preoccupations of young children. But they should. Those early intellectual forays are first steps toward constructing the more powerful and well-developed ideas that are possible later in life. Moreover, the ways that young children assemble (and reassemble) pieces of information forecast the ways that adults put together ideas. Take Bob Kearns, for example. One day, in his early forties, he stopped at a red light while driving in his home city of Detroit. Noting that it had begun to rain lightly, he turned on his windshield wipers. But the switch had only two options, one speed for a regular shower and a faster one for a heavy downpour. In a sparse rain like the one sprinkling his windshield, the wipers screeched and dragged. They made it harder to see, especially given Bob's impaired vision in one eye. Years before, on his wedding night, he had popped the cork from a bottle of champagne, and it had hit him straight in the face. His reflexive blink meant it slammed into his eyelid—otherwise, he might have lost the eye. Sitting at this red light in the rain, he recalled that night in the hotel and thought to himself, "Why can't a windshield wiper work more like an eye?" That unexpected question led him, eventually, to invent a device now so common you've probably never given it one thought—the intermittent windshield wiper. It made him millions of dollars, and the automotive industry millions more. Car buyers today can't imagine buying a vehicle without it. When journalist Josh Seabrook wrote about Kearns, he described the idea as a "flash of genius."[1] But it's not only geniuses who have bright ideas. Anyone can. Ideas come in all shapes and sizes. And they aren't really flashes at all. They're the culmination of a process of gathering and organizing knowledge—the result of days, weeks, or years of thinking about a problem or a possibility, rearranging the pieces of a mental puzzle, and improving one's intellectual plan. The skills and dispositions required for having such ideas take root years before, in early childhood.

Though I didn't know it then, those luscious coffee-table books about Hollywood stars gave me one of my first intellectual projects. It was a meandering undertaking. I had no particular use in mind for the facts I kept sorting, organizing, and mulling over. I wasn't trying to answer a specific question about movie stars and I didn't want to emulate those gorgeous actresses and actors. In fact, many of them made me a little queasy—a bit like those Hostess Snoball treats covered in neon-pink flakes, gross but perpetually tantalizing. Nor was I gathering material for something I wanted to make—a scrapbook, a play, or a collage. I certainly wasn't learning new information that I could use in school.

The truth is, I did it for the sheer pleasure of it. I was an intellectual sybarite. But not all children are so frivolous. Some get swept up by more serious concerns. When Boyan Slat was still just a teenager he learned something that worried him a lot. The world creates over three hundred million tons of plastic each year, and much of that plastic winds up in our rivers, lakes, and oceans. He was appalled by the trend lines showing how severely, within in his lifetime, oceans would be clogged with and degraded by it. Worse yet was the response he got when he raised the issue with adults, even scientists and environmentalists. There was no good solution to the problem, they shrugged. When he was sixteen he went on a scuba-diving trip in Greece, and it was then that the problem became alarmingly real for Slat. As he finned his way through the open water, he saw far more pieces of plastic than sea life floating by. The ocean was teeming with trash. But there, in the deep dark currents, the problem wasn't the only thing that struck him so vividly. So did a possible solution:

I wondered: why move through the oceans if the oceans can move through you? Instead of going after the plastics, you could simply wait for the plastic to come to you, without requiring any added energy. An array of floating barriers would first catch and then concentrate the debris, enabling a platform to efficiently extract the plastic afterwards. The ocean currents would pass underneath these barriers taking . . . sealife with it, preventing by-catch. An elegant idea. But when I got asked to present this idea at the TEDx Delft conference, it wasn't much more than that—an idea.[2]

Slat's ability to seize on a problem and imagine a novel answer didn't spring out of nowhere, once he'd he entered adolescence. Long before he stumbled upon the looming disaster in our oceans, he had begun devising other solutions. An only child, he had spent hours and hours crafting and inventing things. He loved to fashion objects out of wood and assemble devices from everyday materials around the house. When he was just two, he built a chair. Later he built his own treehouse, complete with zip line. His inventions were linked, in his mind, to interesting challenges. When he was fourteen he decided to try and beat the world's record number of water rockets set off at once. Launching 213 water rockets in unison won him a place in the *Guinness Book of World Records*. A host of qualities make young Slat a magnet for media attention and adult admiration. That record and his acclaimed TEDx talk show his tremendous drive, intellectual capacity, and interest in entrepreneurship—and then there's his charmingly floppy hair, the style with which he presents his ideas, and the beautiful English spoken with his native Dutch accent. But all those features that make him a standout young person also obscure the most interesting and important thing about him. What took him from lively minded toddler to eco-entrepreneur was the commitment of time he made looking for puzzles to tackle and coming up with ideas for solutions. It's not that the particular subjects of childhood interests and pastimes foreshadow the areas of adult innovation—it's possible Slat never thought about ocean pollution before he was sixteen, and probably Kearns wasn't interested in windshield wipers as a child. Rather, what took hold when they were little were the processes required to construct such ideas.

A child might be exceptionally smart, overflow with confidence, or have a family that prizes ideas. Some kids, like Slat, enjoy all of these benefits. Most children, however, do not. The majority, by definition, have unexceptional intellectual capacity (with IQs ranging from 85 to 115), and a middling amount of drive. Relatively few are privy to adult discussions of ideas or inventions, and an even smaller number are invited to expand on their own intellectual schemes or musings. But outstanding capacity and extraordinary opportunity are not essential for toddlers and preschoolers to grow into children and adults who pursue ideas. Far more important is the sheer time and attention a child gives, and is encouraged to give, to the consideration of ideas. Every child can learn that building ideas is as tangible, accessible, and alluring as making things with modeling clay. It begins with opportunities to collect information—whether about candy, movie stars, or oceans. And it begins in every kitchen, sidewalk, and kindergarten.

Hiding in Plain Sight

While children are busily gathering information, mulling things over, and speculating about the world, the adults around them are, for the most part, unaware of all that mental activity. Much of the time, they treat children as if they don't have ideas at all. Focused on whether children are learning to behave well, acquiring skills and facts, and feeling happy, they give little consideration to children's thoughts, or the puzzles that intrigue them.

Watch and listen for twenty minutes in almost any school in the United States and it becomes clear that the educational system does not concern itself with children's intellectual lives. This is deeply ironic, since human existence is defined and shaped by the ideas people have had. Waterpiks, contact lenses, and texting have made life much better for so many people. So have psychotherapy, feminism, basketball, the idea of zero, social security, and the Price equation.

While some ideas solve problems, others explain phenomena. In 1976, for example, the biologist Richard Dawkins published *The Selfish Gene,* offering his view of natural selection. It explains how genes, rather than organisms, replicate themselves, giving rise to all kinds of behaviors and characteristics such as length of limbs, eye color, hunting approaches, mating rituals, and food tastes, to name but a microscopic fraction. Dawkins wasn't simply recapitulating Darwin's theory of evolution. This was a new idea, and it caught on like wildfire. He was also fascinated by the huge range of behavioral similarities that could not be explained by genes and might not be rooted in human biology. For example, why do so many people in the United States sing Irving Berlin's "Happy Birthday," wear neckties, and shake the hand of a new acquaintance? These kinds of inherited behaviors could change slightly over time, and eventually be pushed out by replacements. Dawkins argued that such behaviors follow the same pattern as genes—they replicate themselves, and are changed by a combination of chance mutations and the selective pressure of the broader environment. He called these behaviors *memes,* the cultural counterpart to genes. [3] His idea was amazingly influential. Ask anyone under the age of forty to tell you about a meme, and they will readily mention an image or video that has gone viral on social media. Dawkins's proposal, that genes drive biological change and memes drive cultural change, has become more apt than ever. But when Dawkins crafted the idea of memes he wasn't looking to solve a problem exactly. He wanted to explain something—the transmission of behaviors that couldn't be caused by genes. As often as people craft ideas to solve problems (disease, inequity, inefficiency, boredom, and so on), they also build ideas to explain phenomena they can't quite understand.

Daniel Kahneman, whose work on decision-making earned him the Nobel Prize in Economic Sciences, began by noticing a puzzle: Why did people so often make bad decisions, even when the information they needed to make good decisions was right in front of them?[4] Similarly, Leon Festinger developed the idea of cognitive dissonance to make sense of why people often persisted in a belief despite clear evidence it was wrong.[5] It was Claude Steele's insight that "stereotype threat" could explain a baffling pattern of underperformance by Black students on tests of intellectual ability.[6] In all these cases, a new idea made sense of what had made no sense before. Often theories like these are so powerful and pervasive that we no longer even recognize them as ideas. Journalist Stephen Metcalf, for instance, has called neo-liberalism "the idea that swallowed the world," claiming it shapes a thousand and one aspects of everyday life without our even knowing it.[7] Our daily lives rest on good ideas, old and new.

Of course, not all ideas are good. Bad ideas abound. Sometimes it's because they don't work well or adequately explain phenomena. Other times it's because the problems they create are worse than the ones they solve. Topping my list of these would be incarceration, Saran Wrap, and trickle-down economics. However, this book isn't about good ideas versus bad ones. It's about the process of *having* an idea, which is more important and psychologically interesting than the strength or weakness of any particular notion it yields. An idea, whether it's health insurance, democracy, or the microplane, is just the tail end of a mental process that ebbs and flows, however unevenly, throughout a person's waking day. Everyone has ideas now and then—a different way to organize their groceries, a better method of electing presidents, a new insight into why there's a troublemaker in every family. By the age of six, nearly all children have acquired the ingredients necessary to concoct ideas. But by eight, fewer and fewer are doing much concocting. An inventory of the work gathered in al-most any public school classroom, from kindergarten on, will attest to this. You can find lots of evidence that students are honing specific skills and acquiring certain facts. But you will see virtually no sign that they are being given time, support, or guidance to pursue their own original ideas or to investigate the existing ideas that captivate them. This book is about how the process unfolds, and why it matters.

I have spent my entire working life watching children, trying to figure out what's going on inside their minds. I also raised three children of my own. It was obvious from the start that there was much to study about how young children play, express emotions, and make up stories. I had long been interested in their reactions and questions. But I was in my fifties before it dawned on me that they also pursue ideas. Two observations led me there.

The first occurred while I was doing research on children's curiosity. I began to notice that almost all of the studies that examined children's inquiry focused on isolated moments—a child surprised by a worm inching its way across the broccoli, intrigued by the scab that formed on a cut, or mystified about what happened to the sun when it disappeared at night. Experiments on curiosity reflected this short-term, situational view of the phenomenon. We researchers found ways to present our subjects with a surprise (a box that contained a strange object, a film clip of something not seen before) and watched to see what the child did in response.[8] Collectively, we had developed a model that suggested that children's curiosity was always momentary and only incited by something that was happening right there and then. And yet, my observations suggested something quite different. Again and again I noticed children who were dogged in their pursuit of more information on a particular topic. Sometimes the focus of their inquiries was physical: trucks, frogs, or princesses. But sometimes they honed in on more abstract mysteries: politeness, existence, strength. It seemed to me that young children had some big questions on their minds, and that we had paid scant attention to those questions, or their efforts to get answers.

During the same period when I was conducting research on curiosity, my work on education took me to schools, where I spent many hours observing young students, but also parents, teachers, and administrators. I listened carefully to the wide range of things everyone talked about. At some point I began to notice one thing the adults never mentioned: the children's ideas. They discussed the students' family lives and health problems. They spent a great deal of time trying to increase children's self-control, test scores, mental health, and motivation for grades. They mentioned which students were successful and who was headed for trouble. But I never heard any educator discuss what their students were thinking about. When I looked for recent education articles that explored young or older children's ideas, I couldn't find any. I began to realize that adults are largely oblivious to the intellectual lives of young children.

This blind spot is quite strange, since by the time students are in tenth grade, we require them to explain ideas like war, evolution, and regression to the mean. Some teachers even ask them to develop their own ideas about history, literature, science, and math. It struck me that adults seem to believe that when students enter the high school building, they will suddenly, as if by magic, be blessed with the ability to pursue ideas. This makes no sense. Shouldn't we figure out what kinds of ideas they have early on? And then wouldn't it be smart to identify the experiences that would fan the flames of such intellectual activity? Luckily, I realized, psychologists had already gathered much of the data that could shed light on the intellectual lives of children. Past studies only needed to be put together in a new way. This book is about what goes on in the minds of young children. It is also about the conversations, pastimes, and encounters that put them on the path to having more ideas, and stronger ones, as they grow.

My rapt attention to those glossy photos of Gary Cooper and Jean Harlow was a beginning, not an endpoint. When I was thirteen, an English teacher handed me a copy of Thomas Hardy's *Tess of the D'Urbervilles*. Who knows what keen radar told her that, even though the prose was arcane and the themes far outside the realm of my early adolescent experience, I would love it? But I did. For weeks after she handed me the book, I'd slip out of my chair after dinner and retreat to the couch, where I could sink back into its pages—thrilled as much by the depictions of farm life as I was by the heart-wrenching, misguided love between Tess and Angel. Biology, algebra, and history fell away. *The Return of the Native, The Mayor of Casterbridge,* and *Far from the Madding Crowd* stepped forward. It was the second time I experienced the giddy pleasure of realizing that books might come in collections and series—that I didn't always have to regret getting to the end.

Somewhere around that same time, I made my bimonthly trip to stay with my biological father, who lived in New York City. After dinner, as we settled into his living room, he mentioned casually to a dinner guest that he had just reread *The Beast in the Jungle* by Henry James. He said in his slightly musing way, "I always had the thought this story was really about suppressed sexual desire. You know, the genitals were the beast, and the pubic hair was the jungle." I wasn't surprised by his blunt sexual terminology. That was typical of him. What struck me instead was the easy pleasure with which he floated a new idea, as if trying out a fresh literary interpretation was no different from suggesting that we have rice instead of noodles for dinner. I didn't figure out, until years later, that hearing a parent try out an idea was akin to watching a parent bake a cake, or fix a broken machine—all opportunities to do the things grown-ups do, and to learn which activities adults think are valuable.

In March, the same perceptive and lively-minded English teacher who gave me *Tess* decided it was time for me to learn something about writing. She suggested I choose a theme in the Hardy novels and write a "big" paper about it. Other than books, what interested me most right then was that, a few months earlier, I had finally gotten my period. I still looked like a little girl, so menstruation felt like a huge accomplishment. And even though it was still far from the day when I would have one of my own, I thought about romance all the time. So, when I was asked to devote myself to writing about Hardy, the topic appeared in my mind like a movie billboard. I told my teacher I would focus on the way Hardy used nature to talk about sex. I have a vague memory of the quizzical smile on her face. It must have sounded ridiculous, a sheltered girl, not yet fully out of childhood, choosing such a theme. But she didn't reveal even a hint of disdain or disapproval. She cheerily said, "Sounds good to me."

I cringe to think of that final paper. But I also vividly remember writing it. I struggled with figuring out how to parse my big idea into several smaller pieces. It took me time to decide in what order the pieces should go. I can still hear my teacher asking me whether I wanted to present my thoughts in the same sequence they had occurred to me, or some other way. I could reorder an idea? What a revelation. Most of all, I remember the thrill of returning to pages deep in the novels, to find passages that would support my hunch. I remember the joy of discovering that as I wrote, new thoughts occurred. My idea had legs.

2

Inquiry

How come wherever I go, something is happening?

—Four-year-old child, from archived conversation in the Child Language Data Exchange System (CHILDES)

The first leaf was large and vermillion. It was bigger than Addie's hand and its width was greater than both of her hands put together, which were the wrong size and shape for carrying such a treasure—her fingers far too chubby and short. She had no way of grasping the leaf without crushing it. Luckily it had a handle of sorts—a long supple stem, easy to grip. The stem ran through the middle of the leaf like a spine, with veins branching out on both sides, almost all the way to the edges, where they seemed to fade. Addie didn't spend much time admiring it. She wanted to keep walking. It was more of a trot, really, which was the only way she could keep up with her companions, who had much longer legs. Clutching the stem and letting the brilliant leaf membrane glow and wave in the breeze like a small flag, she hustled forward. The tree trunks towered over her so tall that, as far as she was concerned, they rose up indefinitely into the sky. But she didn't look up much. She was intent on scanning the ground around her. The others noticed that she seemed to be walking with great purpose, though it wasn't clear what that purpose was. The others were simply following a well-worn path, which made a loop around a small lake. Eventually they'd be back at the beginning. Why did Addie seem to be striding forward in such a businesslike way? What did she have in mind?

Two minutes further into the walk, Addie crouched down, close to the ground. She didn't have far to go. She briskly reached out and retrieved another fallen leaf, a little damp from the wet earth, this one a vivid crimson. With no hesitation, she held it up in one hand, alongside the original leaf in the other, and studied the two selections. After several seconds of careful consideration, she decisively flung the second leaf back to the ground, stood up, and resumed her trot forward. About fifty feet later, she spied another candidate, squatted down again, held up the new leaf, subjected it to her side-by-side scrutiny, and rejected it, as well. By the time the three hikers—two adults plus the two-year-old Addie—had made their way around the lake, she had compared the original leaf to eighteen others, only to conclude that the original one, so large, orange-red, and magnificent, could not be topped.

Yet she did keep one more leaf, a deep ruby red one, smaller than the first but also perfectly shaped. Once she was lifted into her car seat and strapped in safely, she held one leaf stem in each stubby fist, looking back and forth from one to the other, as the car traveled toward her house. Not yet three, she had curated a collection. But the beginnings of her close comparison and study had taken root two years before, in her first moments of life.

Surprises

Babies are born equipped with a novelty detector. They notice, almost from birth, any new object or event that comes within view or earshot. Research suggests that the infant becomes familiar in utero with its birth mother's vocal tones and cadences. Soon after birth, most babies start responding differently when people other than their caregivers talk to them. Within months, whenever they see something different from what they have seen before, their heart rate changes, their breath quickens, and their skin produces more moisture—all signs that they have taken notice. Shown a series of images of a particular face projected on a screen, infants quickly grow tired of looking. They learn the face easily and then have little interest in it. But present them with the image of a different, new face and they will study it for several seconds.[1] They notice the discrepancy. It's not just that they detect novelty. That's only the starting point.

They are driven, instinctively, to study unfamiliar objects, people, and events in order to make the new familiar. Presented with visual patterns or images, babies look longer at the one they have never seen before. They absorb new phenomena, looking and listening until something is no longer surprising. But they quickly go beyond using just their ears and eyes. Soon enough, babies expand their investigative repertoire to include touching, grasping, licking, and mouthing. By the time they are several months old, they reach out for things, pounding, shaking, and kicking to discover features of new objects.

Not only do babies have exquisite radar for the unfamiliar, they also come equipped with a strong impulse to investigate whatever unexpected objects and events they encounter. It's their way of reducing uncertainty, using whatever exploration strategies possible. Because their daily lives bring them face to face with a relentless stream of new sights and sounds, babies and toddlers lean, nearly constantly, on this powerful pair of intellectual tools. Is the fact that their days are crammed with investigation important to development?

To answer that question, you need only take stock in the most cursory way of the differences between a newborn baby and a toddler. Human babies seem pathetically helpless by the standards of other mammals, who walk and nourish themselves within hours of birth. And yet, by their third year, humans make use of a dazzling array of knowledge and skills never available to the smartest dog, mouse, or pig. The newborn cries and makes vegetative noises; the typical three-year-old talks in full sentences, carries on complex conversations, refers to the past and the future, and tells intricate stories that include characters, plots, and surprise endings. The newborn can merely look, listen, and grasp; the three-year-old can take things apart, put them together, build towers, enact dramas, and draw pictures. The newborn shows interest in those around her, but often in a seemingly vague and detached way—she smiles with pleasure when her father talks to her, or cries in fear at the approach of a strange person. By three, however, she has mastered a wide range of social skills: she knows when someone is pretending and when those same actions are for real, she knows how to persuade and lie, she understands the difference between family and not family, and she is likely to have a formidable lexicon of social dos and don'ts. Toddlers also have an impressive repertoire of scripts—they know what to expect for breakfast, how dogs behave, what a trip to the grocery store entails, the route to day care—and at least passing familiarity with thousands of objects, people, and events that crop up in their daily lives.[2] What accounts for the breathtaking rate and scope of knowledge acquisition that happens during the first years of life? What is the motor driving this superb learning machine? The answer lies in children's urge to reduce uncertainty and explain the unexpected. Surprise, and babies' overpowering need to resolve it, explains how helpless infants who merely burp, gurgle, kick, and cry become savvy members of the community in just three years. Curiosity is the psychological foundation that explains the vast terrain of knowledge and skills acquired, apparently effortlessly, by virtually all typically developing children.[3]

But the endless barrage of surprises and mysteries doesn't last forever. By the age of three, the child has a huge working knowledge of everyday routines and environments. Much has become comfortably familiar, such as what will be on the breakfast table, the kinds of things family members typically do and say, what they will see at the grocery store, what is involved in bath time, and what happens when there is a birthday. At this point, a subtle but profound change occurs in the inner lives of most children. They begin to take an active role in choosing which surprises to notice and pursue. The everyday world becomes the familiar background to more distinctive events and objects, which call out for further explanation and mastery. Imagine, for instance, a boy of eighteen months going for the first time to a zoo. Any number of things might be equally riveting—the booth where his grandfather buys the admission tickets; the seals in their pool, diving, bobbing, and slinging themselves onto rock ledges; another child having a crying fit over a dropped ice cream cone; a pigeon pecking a small pile of garbage; and the large gorilla, sitting solemn and heavy in his habitat, staring out disapprovingly at the young viewers. Perhaps, after all, the boy is most intrigued by jumping over a puddle of water at the entrance to the primate building. Now imagine that same child two years later. Many elements of a zoo have become routine—ticket booths, pigeons (if he lives in the city), puddles, and other children crying. Some elements may not be regular parts of his everyday life. But he has visited the zoo many times, looked at books about animals, and, between movies, television shows, and YouTube clips, watched numerous live-action sequences about seals, gorillas, and other creatures that don't live in his immediate environment. What will surprise him enough now to elicit his gaze, sustained observation, questions, or some other type of investigation? This depends, in part, on his own particular interests.

From Surprise to Investigation

By age four, everyday routines cause little surprise for children, and little or no fodder for their curiosity. At this point, children are ready to be somewhat choosier. They begin to play a more active role in deciding what aspects of daily life they can skim over, and which to zero in on. While virtually all eighteen-month-olds seem inquisitive throughout the great majority of their waking day, the four-year-old is likely to seem blasé about many aspects of daily life. Lunch, the trip to preschool, regular visits from a grandmother, and the habits of the family pet are as humdrum to them as they are to us—features of life that only surprise us in their absence or when those routines and routine creatures do something out of the ordinary. It is during this period, when daily life becomes mundane, that most children develop very specific interests. One becomes fascinated with bugs, another intent on listening and watching when people laugh or fight with one another, and a third with anything mechanical—small gadgets, machines, and puzzles. Needless to say, children's interests don't always boldly announce themselves. For every child who makes it clear they are obsessed by dinosaurs there is another child whose interests are subtler and more oblique—the child who notices the way small things are put together, or listens intently to the words other people use, quickly absorbing unusual and interesting terms they've never heard before. But whether their interests are vivid and palpable, or lie invisible under the surface, such preoccupations provide a guiding force throughout a child's waking day.

In 1883, the American psychologist G. Stanley Hall published a classic article, now nearly forgotten: "The Contents of Children's Minds on Entering School."[4] His report begins by describing the results of a study carried out in Germany in 1869–1870, in which teachers across the city of Berlin were invited to interview the children arriving in their classrooms on a wide range of topics, assessing their awareness of their father's business, their understanding of the firmament, and their familiarity with things like a mushroom, a plow, the evening sky, a triangle, a pleasure garden, and a "park for invalids"—to name just a few of the seventy-five items on the protocol. Using this as a basis to investigate children's "ideas" in his own country, Hall asked teachers in Kansas and Boston to interview their students on a somewhat similar set of topics he devised. Much of his list was made up of questions like which was the left hand and which was the right one, what quantity various numbers referred to, and how sewing was done—testing what might be called basic knowledge rather than probing what was on the children's minds or the nature of their ideas. Analyzing the data he got back, Hall reported patterns of differences between children who lived in the city and those from rural areas, between boys and girls, and between those who had attended kindergarten and those who had not. His questions probed children's knowledge of all sorts of flora and fauna (such as oak tree, buttercup, moss, worm, snail, and sheep), various kinds of natural events (storms, moonrise, sunrise), and particular trades (how leather is made, how watchmakers work, what bricks are made of). He had teachers report how many Bible stories children knew, and how many Grimm's fairy tales. His odd combination of particular bits of information with more general kinds of knowledge and core skills limits the usefulness of his data to contemporary scholars. And yet, his wide and eclectic survey affords a glimpse into what aspects of daily life his young subjects paid attention to and what they ignored or missed. Looking at Hall's data now, one isn't convinced that he actually plumbed the contents of children's minds. But he did point the way to an important idea: that children's interests vary, and their interests greatly influence what they know. The line of inquiry he opened up would eventually prove productive. It lay dormant for nearly fifty years, however—and when it did resurface, the work wasn't even, initially, about children.

In the late 1950s and 1960s, Daniel Berlyne did a series of experiments showing that adults remember information better when that information has piqued their curiosity. He found that surprising or odd information piqued the adults' interest, causing them to attend to it more fully and, as a result, retain it longer and more accurately.[5] More recently, researchers have provided additional data showing that people explore more fully when there is something they want to find out. Christopher Hsee and Bowen Ruan, for example, recruited adults to participate in a study and when each arrived, he or she was ushered into a "waiting room" from which they would be called in a short while. All were told that, while they were waiting, they should feel free to check out the prank pens that were material for another study. For half the subjects, there were five red pens and five green pens in the room, and their host mentioned that, while the red ones had batteries installed and would therefore deliver a tiny shock when clicked, the green pens did not. For the other half, there were ten yellow pens, and subjects were told only that some of them would deliver a shock. The subjects in the latter group clicked significantly more pens than those presented with the red and green mix. In other words, uncertainty led to exploration—what Hsee and Ruan termed the "Pandora effect."[6]

If adults explore further and learn more when faced with surprise or mystery, what about children? Studies have shown just how powerful the bug of uncertainty is in motivating children to seek information. In one study, Laura Schulz and Elizabeth Bonawitz showed preschoolers a "machine." It was a box with two levers on the side; one made a toy duck pop out and the other a puppet. In one condition, the experimenter pressed one of the levers at the same time that the child pressed the other lever, so that it was impossible to figure out which lever controlled the duck and which controlled the puppet. In a second condition, the experiment pressed a lever before or after the child did, so that it quickly became clear which lever caused which toy to pop out. Children spent more time playing with the box in the first condition, when the causal structure of the toy was ambiguous.[7] The findings add to a host of other recent studies showing that curiosity drives learning. Claire Cook and her colleagues gave four-year-olds a chance to investigate a toy machine that lit up when an experimenter used certain beads to touch the surface, and didn't light up when other beads, or bead combinations, were used. In one condition, the pattern was clear and it was easy to figure out which bead combinations would activate the lights. In a second condition, the evidence was more ambiguous. The children in the ambiguous condition were much more likely to continue playing with the machine. Uncertainty drew them in, the researchers concluded; children want to discover the cause of things.[8] Other recent studies have shown that, as young as age three, children can grasp the difference between a good causal link and a bad one.

Rachel Magid and her colleagues showed young children one of two visual effects on the screen of a desktop computer disguised as a "big machine." In one condition, children saw a spinning, rainbow-colored ball move diagonally from the bottom left corner to the top right corner of the screen and back again—a *continuous* effect. In the other condition, they saw a static image of the same ball appear in the bottom left corner, then in the top right, then back in the bottom left—a *discrete* effect. The machine also featured a "controller" with two parts. One of these was a "wheel" switch that could be dialed up or down in any increment, and the other was a choice of two metal squares where the child could stick a magnet. Each child was given the chance to manipulate the parts of the controller while it was "unplugged" and then watched while the experimenter plugged it in and set up a cloth screen that made it impossible to see how the controller was being used. One of the two previously viewed effects appeared on the screen. Then, the child was asked to guess which part of the controller the experimenter had used. Most children who saw the discrete display (the ball appearing in one corner and then reappearing in another corner) believed the experimenter had used the magnet with its two discrete choices, and most children who saw the ball glide continuously across the screen thought the experimenter had rolled the wheel. In other words, they made an abstract connection between the kind of cause and the kind of effect.[9] Studies like this show that children not only seek explanations, they seek good ones. Given an opportunity to identify the cause of something ambiguous, they're eager to do it, and they're not bad at it. But, as Hall showed over a century ago, not all puzzles are equally fascinating to all children. By the time they are three, their specific interests are as important as the inherent mystery of an object or an event. Do their interests follow any kind of pattern? Research has uncovered some, though not all, of the answers to this.

In one study led by Deborah Kelemen, researchers interviewed a group of mothers about all the conversations they had had with their children over a two-week period. The researchers were interested in the type of explanations mothers offered in response to their children's questions. In particular, they wanted to know how often mothers provided what psychologists call causal explanations (it's raining because there were clouds in the sky, and then it got warmer), as opposed to teleological explanations (it's raining because the flowers need it to grow). But the conversations also show that children were far more interested in some kinds of information than others—they especially liked to get explanations about animals and humans. They were much less drawn to conversations about the inanimate natural world (mountains, for instance) and the non-natural world (machines, for instance).[10]

My own lab has collected data suggesting a similar pattern. We invited children between the ages of five and seven to look at several collages and pick which they'd like to look at more and talk about. One collage depicted animals, another people, and a third machines and gadgets. Overwhelmingly, the children were most interested in looking at and talking about the animals. Their second favorite was the collage of people, and the machine collage came in last place. It seems that, in this culture, at least, there are some broad trends in what grabs children's interest. Things that are sentient, unpredictable, and to some degree, like us, are what we most want to know more about. But these general patterns don't tell the whole story, either. Because as any parent can tell you, what might seem humdrum to one child is riveting to another.

What Children Want to Know

Though all children are intrigued by surprise and ambiguity, there is remarkable variety in children's particular interests. When we showed children the animal collage, some wanted to know more about sea creatures, and others about big cats. In 1996, Stacey Baker and James Gentry interviewed seventy-nine first- and fifth-graders to learn more about children's collections. Seventy-two of the children they interviewed said they had at least one collection. Many of the older children seemed to focus on the sheer pleasure of acquisition, but that was less true of younger children. In fact, many of them mentioned the way in which their collections helped satisfy their curiosity. The interviewers asked one boy why he collected live frogs. He answered, "Because I always find something new every time I look. . . . It makes me more interested." Describing her collection of plastic and glass horses, one girl said, "I find information about horses in like catalogs, magazines, and stores when we go there. I can remember like, look at a horse and remember when I got it and who gave it to me, stuff like that. . . . I spend a lot of time thinking about horses."[11] These answers provide a vital clue about the topics that elicit children's interest beyond the moment. When children collect information over time, whether through objects, pictures in a book, or experiences, it is almost always because the topic presents puzzles, offers a mystery that needs solving, or in some other way provokes a desire for explanation.

When Addie rushed about on the lake path, finding and comparing leaves, she was not just seeking information. She was seeking information to settle a question, however implicit and undeveloped her question may have been. It's not easy to ascertain what question motivated her seeking behavior, since toddlers are unlikely to articulate their questions clearly, even to themselves. Perhaps she wanted to find out something about their various sizes—what the biggest the leaf might be, and what the smallest. Perhaps she was interested in the gradation of hue and tone from one leaf to another. Whatever details or points of comparison she sought, her fledgling collecting behavior hints at an important feature of young children's emerging intellectual lives. The world doesn't simply foist surprise on the young, inexperienced mind. Children aren't simply stumbling from one unexpected event in the world to another, haplessly responding to whatever comes their way. Even the two-year-old mind is actively building up stores of knowledge about the particular things that interest her. By noticing a discrepancy, a similarity, or a pattern, the child creates his or her own new mystery—the more she knows about a domain, the more able she is to notice small sources of surprise, which in turn leads to greater knowledge. Lifting leaves and holding them up to one another is one way to seek information. But by the middle of their third year, most children have a new and uniquely powerful tool for probing topics—one that distinguishes them from all other primates. They ask questions.

The psychologist Michelle Chouinard examined a huge corpus of questions asked by four young children, who were regularly recorded at home from their third year until they were five. In total she took stock of over 24,741 questions, recorded over 229.5 hours of interaction. One of the children, referred to by researchers as Adam, asked more than 10,905 questions during the fifty-five hours his talk was recorded (or to think of it a different way, Adam asked about 198 questions per hour, over three per minute). In contrast, one of the other young subjects, referred to as Sarah, asked 6,296 questions during nearly seventy hours of data collection. Sarah's rate of question asking was less than half of Adam's. Even so, she asked, on average, just over one question per minute. They asked questions for all kinds of reasons, including to get attention, to seek permission, and to request some action from an adult. But more than seventy percent of their questions reflected a desire for information. At three, they sought specific facts about the social and physical world around them, asking questions such as *What's that?* or *Where's the ball?* But by the time the children were five, they also wanted many explanations for events, objects, and conversations that perplexed them: *Why is the baby crying? Why is the cereal hot? Why don't we see two things with our two eyes? How do you make it go over there?*[12]

At one year of age, virtually none of a child's questions seek explanations. But by the time they pass their fifth birthday, nearly a third of the questions they ask are aimed at finding out *why* and *how*. Children of this age find surprise in all kinds of seemingly minor daily events: one child asks why ice cubes turn to water, another wants to know why some dogs bark and others don't, and a third wonders about old people why they have wrinkles, why their teeth are yellow, and why they use canes. Young children use questions to collect whatever information matters most to them, and thus their questions provide us with a window onto their intellectual preoccupations.

It's easy for adults to glide over the wealth of information contained in a young child's questions. And yet, knowing that there is a surprising range of questions they *can* ask makes the questions they *do* ask all the more revealing. Some evidence for the possibilities within the question-asking system comes from comparisons of children in different cultures. Mary Gauvain and her colleagues recorded young children's questions in four places—Belize, Kenya, Nepal, and American Samoa—and compared their data with Chouinard's. Children in those four communities asked a great many questions, just as the US children did. However, the proportion of those questions aimed at getting explanations was far lower.[13] It seems that US children want to know some things children in other cultures find less interesting, or at least less appropriate to ask about.

In trying to figure out why US children ask for explanations so much more often than the children in these other four cultures, Gauvain and her colleagues provide the following example of a US child's tenacious efforts to get an explanation for a social mystery:

Mother: He's a little boy who's painting.
Child: Why he painting?
Mother: Because he likes to paint.
Child: Why he like to paint?
Mother: Because it's fun.
Child: Why it's fun?
Mother: Because it's something he likes to do.
Child: Why he like to do it?[14]

Is it that US children find such matters more interesting than their peers in other cultures do, or is it that they are less inhibited in their questioning? The authors point out that children in Samoa, Nepal, Belize, and Kenya are expected to honor a certain distance between adults and children. Questions that seek explanations (*why* questions) might appear insolent in such communities. For children in those cultures, it may therefore feel safer to stick to a higher proportion of questions seeking permission, the names of things, and the correct way to do things. Whatever the cause of the difference, the effect is likely to be powerful: children in the US hear a great many explanations for things at a very early age. More than that, we know that children's curiosity is most directed at their particular nascent interests, so these early question-and-answer exchanges with parents assist them in shaping their subsequent ideas.

For instance, Meredith Rowe and her colleagues analyzed conversations between US fathers and their young children. They examined the questions fathers asked their toddlers, and then studied those same children a few years later. The children whose fathers had asked more *why* and *how* questions when they had just learned to talk knew more and showed higher-level cognitive functioning when they were in preschool.[15] This adds to the growing consensus among researchers that even the most casual exchanges between parents and young children have strong, long-lasting impacts on the children's minds. Questions provide children with a unique tool for acquiring the answers they want. But these knowledge-building exchanges can provide more than the particular information being sought. The implication of Rowe's data is that the nature of the questions asked and answered at home has a formative influence on the habits of thinking that children acquire—specifically, that more early exposure to *why* and *how* lays a foundation for greater capacity to think along logical lines. There was already powerful evidence that children who grow up in families that talk a lot are more likely to do well in school later on, and conversely, that children who hear fewer words at home struggle at school.[16] Beyond that basic, crude distinction, studies have also shown that it's not merely the sheer quantity of words that fuels the child's mind, but also the way words are used. Children who live in families that chat, reminisce, and share feelings and perceptions learn differently than children whose families use language simply to conduct daily life (for instance, to give instructions or chastise).[17] Researchers have also known for some time now that children who engage in longer conversations more frequently have an easier time learning to read.[18] By conversing about the world around them, children seem to prepare for the kind of thinking required to read about the wide range of experiences captured in print: distant places, unknown people, and far-off events. The lesson from Rowe's data is that certain kinds of questions asked and encouraged of children at home open up additional intellectual doors. The kinds of questions that surround children can also teach them that knowledge is worth seeking, and that intellectual pursuits are valuable. Questions that add information to an emerging constellation of knowledge help children develop the capacity and disposition to *think* about knowledge, rather than just *use* it.

A striking demonstration of this can be gleaned from a collection of studies showing that children who grow up in religious communities are less likely to think critically about new information than children who grow up in atheist families. Specifically, children who grow up in atheistic families are more likely to seek evidence and reasons when presented with unfamiliar data or novel arguments.[19] One interpretation is that children who are raised to believe that the answers to some of life's greatest mysteries must be taken on faith are less likely in general to see the value of questioning what they are told. The way children perceive adults approaching and talking about the world matters deeply. It shapes not only what children believe and know, but also the extent to which their beliefs and knowledge will grow.

But maturation also has a hand in the kinds of things young children ask about. We've seen that children's first questions tend to seek the names and locations of things (*who, what,* and *where*). Then, by the time they have turned three, children use questions to seek explanations (*why* and *how*). Psychologists refer to these questions as *epistemic*—borrowing Aristotle's term for thinking about the durable facts of the world's workings. But much of the research on epistemic curiosity has focused on children's responses to concrete objects and single moments in time—as when an animal makes an unexpected noise, an unusual object is produced that the child has never seen before, or a substance behaves in an unforeseen way. In such studies, the child's curiosity is piqued by an obvious surprise and resolved by an observable response in just a few minutes. But not all curiosities announce themselves so noticeably or prove so fleeting.

Generating Curiosity

When Addie collected the leaves, she wasn't just seeking information, she was also creating a need for it, carving out her own intellectual terrain. Collecting those leaves took her just a little while—the whole process was completed within forty minutes. She carried out many such brief collecting forays—sea glass one afternoon at the beach, dead flies in her grandmother's kitchen, small branches after a storm near her home, and on one cold afternoon, icicles plucked from the edge of the porch where she lived. But by the time she was four, those frequent but brief bursts of collecting had prepared the way for something more sustained. It seemed to begin one hot day in June when Addie and her father left the house on their way to day care. As Addie walked out the door, she nearly stepped on a large, shiny, dark brown beetle. She was barefoot at the time, insistent, as usual, that her father wait until just before she was lifted out of her car seat for the walk to her classroom to put on the very small, very bright orange Crocs she wore in warm weather. Her small, squat foot, its sole covered with an impressive layer of dirt, was already scarred from past accidental encounters with sharp edges, heavy rocks, and splintery planks. Now it was lined up side by side and very, very close to the hairy-looking leg of a june bug. Addie stopped short and gazed with rapt attention as the creature's two antennae began to move and its legs went into action. Then, scanning the porch floor just beyond it, she saw more creatures just like it milling around, their motion strangely dreamlike, yet industrious. Her eyes shot back to the first bug and her leg slid over a bit, to the point that her small foot just touched the bug's metallic shell. Her father, barely registering Addie's interest, took her hand to lead her toward the car and said vaguely, to no one in particular, "Gotta sweep those up."

"Sweep?" Addie asked as her father buckled her in.

"Huh?" he replied absently.

"You said sweep up. Sweep up what?"

"Oh, right, the june bugs. I hope I remember to sweep 'em up when I get home tonight."

"They're dirty?" said Addie.

"No, but they're a pain. No one wants a june bug flying into them."

"They fly?" Addie's eyes widened slightly. But by then, her father was in the driver's seat and they were headed toward the road. Addie looked out the window, watching the trees rush by. Fifteen minutes later, she arrived at her classroom and happily joined a small group of pals who were planning a house they wanted to build with the large cardboard boxes in the corner. Her moment with june bugs had passed. Or so it seemed.

A few days later, Addie and her friends were seated at one of the low tables built just for three-year-olds, eating the food they had each brought from home. As they discussed which of them would be brave enough to swim in very cold water, Addie noticed something move on the corner of the table. She had been eating the chunks of melon her father had packed for her. Now, her cheeks bulging with fruit, a slight dribble of melon juice rolling toward her chin, she paused her chewing to watch an insect make its zig-zagging way toward her melon container.

"June bug!" she announced. Her teacher was standing nearby.

"Nope. That's not a june bug, Miss Addie. That's an ant. She wants to share your melon. You girls have made quite a mess, haven't you? A feast for these nasty bugs." Addie's gaze stayed fixed on the insect.

"But does he fly?"

By the time children are two, many show a particular interest in the natural world, especially the world of animals and animal behavior. Research by Susan Carey, among other psychologists, shows that this intense interest in animals stems in part from children's natural and intuitive grasp of core biological concepts, such as the difference between animate and inanimate entities.[20] But this is only a beginning. Whatever their innate tendencies might draw them to, young children have many options for where to spend their learning time and energy. For one study, Chouinard equipped parents of 112 preschoolers with small, portable recording devices and arranged for each parent-child pair to visit a nearby zoo, and asked the parents to record everything that happened while they were there. The children in this study asked even more questions (on average, ninety-five per hour) than similar children studied in other settings. Analysis of the questions suggests that children become more directed in their curiosity as they get older; whereas about twenty percent of the youngest children's questions were part of a focused series in which each question built on the last, this was true of nearly half the questions from four-year-olds.

Some interests seem to elicit more targeted searches than others, and the topic of animals is high on that list.[21] Thomas Beery and Kristi

Lekies asked five thousand undergraduates to answer questions about their collecting habits as children. The overwhelming majority, nearly 88 percent, remembered collecting specimens from outside when they were between the ages of three and ten. Some categories were more popular than others: approximately 30 percent remembered collecting objects such as leaves, feathers, seeds, sticks, mushrooms, fruits and berries, fossils, and insects. It's worth noting that many of those surveyed recalled surprisingly specific details of their childhood collections, even though they were adults:

> "I caught live eels in the shallows from time to time, though they were let loose after five to ten minutes."
> "Some of them looked like emeralds, big green rocks."[22]

They must have paid plenty of attention to objects within the collection, noting all kinds of details, creating long-lasting and vivid impressions.

It's possible, however, that asking adults what they recall of their childhood collections may slant the data. The act of remembering oneself as a child may add a sense of focus and thoroughness to an activity or experience that it lacked at the time. A few scattered episodes may take on a significance or coherence in retrospect. And yet, when parents are asked to describe their young children's collections, their answers align with what those college students remembered. Children seem extra interested in the natural world, and that interest extends beyond sentient beings. A young colleague who lives in Maryland shares this report on her four-year-old Alma's gatherings:

> Alma has been collecting rocks and shells for over a year, since she turned three. Sometimes she goes weeks without adding to the collection, and it seems she's forgotten all about it. But then

one day we'll get home from an expedition to the park or to visit her cousins, and her pockets will be filled with new stones, or a small shell. She doesn't do anything with her shells and rocks. She just keeps them in a corner in her room. After she's found a new one she'll usually add it to the pile, and then she usually spends quite a bit of time going over the collection—just touching the different ones, talking quietly to herself. When I get close enough, I can hear her murmuring, "very smooth, rough, a little bumpy." Sometimes after she finds a new one, she'll reorganize them all into separate little piles, based on their texture, or their size. Every once in a while, someone will offer her a rock or a shell for her collection. She doesn't accept them all. Only the ones that "fit," whatever that means to her.

When does interest like Alma's become more focused and directed? When does the young collector become the young researcher? Using a large corpus of questions asked by children between the ages of one and five, Chouinard and her colleagues looked at when children shift from asking questions that jump from one topic to another to using questions to dive deeper. When children first ask questions (some with words and some with gestures), 97 percent refer to an isolated topic, which is to say the inquiry does not extend beyond one question. Common phrases include *What is that? What does it do?* and *What's that called?* Children appear to be casting a wide net, collecting bits and pieces of information about a vast array of things. By the time they are four and a half, however, their questions are equally divided between single questions on a topic and question series that pursue lines of inquiry.[23]

In her analysis of the four children over time, Chouinard looked at the questions they asked just after turning one year old. Fully 87 percent of these questions were "one-offs"—single questions about isolated topics. Then she looked at questions asked after their fifth birthdays. Things had changed: now only 37 percent were stand-alone queries, while 63 percent combined to pursue a topic further. This led Chouinard to a next question of her own. She hypothesized that, if children use questions to collect a broad range of information as a first step toward seeking deeper understanding, then the kinds of questions children asked might change as they moved to the next step of building up knowledge. To test this, she examined the questions children used when they stuck with something. She found that, indeed, the usual approach was for preschoolers to begin by asking stand-alone questions that allowed them to gather facts. The children's opening gambits were about all manner of topics, including dogs, the weather, and people's behavior. Once they had collected a bit of *what* information, they began to ask more probing *why* and *how* questions about those initial facts.[24] In Chouinard's data is the evidence that even preschoolers use an intellectual strategy to satisfy their curiosities. Their many questions may come across as scattershot but, in fact, they follow a pattern.

Certainly, that was true for Addie. During her fourth year, Addie's life was filled with bugs. She spent at least a little time every week talking about bugs and looking at them in pictures, books, and real life. Periodically she had the chance to actually touch one, or even catch it and investigate further. Those examinations were sporadic, and while some lasted just a minute, others stretched to twenty minutes. During the warm summer months, bugs were a part of nearly every day. There were ants, beetles, stink bugs, silverfish, and myriad flying insects—black flies, wasps, deerflies, and bees. Among a few highlights, there was the day her father knocked down a hornet's nest from the edge of the garage. There was the unsettling but enthralling time she watched her mother use tweezers to detach a tick from her leg. Almost as good as seeing her jerk it out and burn it was hearing her talk about the danger of Lyme disease. Addie was more intrigued than nervous. How could something so tiny make you sick? And how exactly *did* it make you sick? And then there was the confusing moment a neighbor pointed out an insect whose slim body had what looked like four bent twigs sticking out of it. It was called a water strider, the neighbor explained, because it could stay up on the surface of the pond. It was a revelation that there were bugs that could float and swim, as well as fly, creep, and scurry.

For a while, Addie couldn't get enough information about bugs. But as the cool weather blew in, her attention waned. There were fewer of them around, and other problems just begged to be solved—kickball, reading, and a new little girl who had joined her school. Then, in November, her brother showed her a *National Geographic* issue that had an extreme close-up of a dragonfly on the cover. It appeared to have a brilliant green mask covering its eyes and cheeks, and leaving its pale, spongy-looking face bulging out in the middle. It was disgusting and scary, something like one of the small plastic supervillains her brother owned, which she so loved to play with. She couldn't stop looking at the picture of the repulsive and impressive dragonfly. Her preoccupation with bugs, dormant since summer's end, resurfaced.

She held on to the magazine for a week, peering at it now and then between other activities. For several days it was tucked near the toilet. But she didn't just peruse and study. She also periodically peppered her family members with questions: *Can a fly make you sick like a tick? Do the ants eat my cereal? Is that stuff its poop? Do they fight? How do they know how to make a line?* (this last in response to a long string of ants marching to and from a piece of cookie lying on the kitchen floor).

And then there were the experiments. One day in August, when her grandmother launched into her annual vigorous hunt for flies, armed with an old, orange plastic flyswatter, Addie decided she'd take a turn. Her first six or seven attempts were misses. Then, with great concentration, she quietly crept up to a large black fly on the kitchen table, and with all her power, smacked down the swatter. A hit. She lifted up the swatter, and found the fly, dead and not too smooshed, lying on the table. As delicately as she could, she pinched it between her short, chubby fingers and brought it very close to her face. Her eyes widened. It had the same kind of shiny eye mask that the dragonfly wore, only this mask was black, not green. Also like the dragonfly, the middle of the fly's face was made of something spongy. Better yet, it appeared to have hair on its body. Then one of the spindly legs moved. She had thought it was dead and would remain inert, the way all bugs did when her grandmother swatted them. She dropped it back onto the table and watched to see if the leg would move again. That's when her grandmother, who had been cleaning nearby, looked over, grabbed the flyswatter, smacked it again, and threw it out. The experiment was over.

Another day, as she and her friend Mae wandered around the lawn discussing the possibility of mermaids, she saw a cluster of bugs clambering over a very small item that looked vaguely familiar. She called to her friend, "Hey. Mae. Mae. Look." The two girls bent over to see what it could be that was so covered in bugs. It was a piece of ham, fallen from a sandwich eaten earlier in the day. Mae suggested they enlist the family dog. "Pickle'll eat 'em! See if he'll eat 'em. Here, Pickle. Want a nice little treat?" The girls watched with disgusted delight, as the obliging Labrador sniffed and pushed the bit of meat with his nose. Addie said with glee, "Yeah, Pickle. Don't you wanna eat some nice little ants?" The girls tilted forward expectantly as Pickle nudged the piece of ham again, but just then he turned away, no longer interested.

To a casual passerby, this incident would not have looked at all consequential. Two children milling around, temporarily engrossed by some ants and a chance to play with the family dog. It certainly wouldn't have been clear that the moment was connected in any way to Addie's ongoing interest in insects, or general need to find out more. But the passerby would have been wrong. However sporadic these bug encounters, they provided Addie with a steady stream of information. Her curiosity about bugs unfolded over a few years, and in stages her focus shifted: at first she found the features and actions of the june bug absorbing; later, she wanted to know more of the specific capabilities of various insects; and by the time she was four, she was drawing more general conclusions about insect life—their variations and similarities, their behavior patterns, and even their vulnerabilities. Addie was becoming something of a bug aficionado.

The Force of Expertise

In the early 1980s, Micheline Chi and her colleagues set out to put their finger on just what it is that "develops" in children's thinking. When a child achieves a change in capacity or way of doing things—say, memory improves or it becomes easier to understand certain ideas—what exactly has undergone development?[25] Up until that moment, most twentieth-century developmental cognitive psychologists had accepted a framework laid out by that great pioneer of child cognitive development, Jean Piaget. According to it, children's thinking underwent broad changes at certain critical junctures: two-year-olds began thinking in symbols, five-year-olds could think about the world and not just act on it, seven-year-olds could to some degree understand abstractions, and so on.[26] The picture of cognitive growth over time was compelling, but did not explain what mechanism in children's experience might serve to catapult them into each next stage of mental capability with its new ways of thinking. Piaget rejected the idea that maturation alone explained mental development. He argued instead that a child's interactions with the world fueled the change. But it was never clear how those interactions accounted for the dramatic developmental changes that children everywhere, no matter how they grew up, experienced.

Then, in the 1970s and 1980s, computers became mainstream. Psychologists discovered that the workings of these new machines provided a marvelous analog for the developing mind. By figuring out what input the computer needed to carry out various tasks, the researchers could build a model of what the developing child might need to know in order to master an activity and they could also model how the child might approach the task, step by step.[27]

This in turn suggested to researchers what it is that changes, as children's thinking (and the behavior it leads to) grows more sophisticated. Chi led an important series of studies showing that how much a child knows about something is intricately tied to what we think of as their "developmental level."[28] In a famous line of inquiry, she and her colleagues showed that young children who were dinosaur experts (which characterizes more than a few five-year-olds) employed more advanced thinking skills when answering dinosaur-related questions than they did in addressing other kinds of problems—and that they were more advanced than other children their age who were dinosaur novices, though similar in all other ways. In one study, seven-year-olds were first quizzed with flashcards and a set of eighteen dinosaur fact questions (for instance: *The name Brontosaurus means what kind of lizard?*). Scores on this pretest were used to sort the children into two groups: experts and novices.[29] Next, the researchers asked the children (in both groups) to look at the cards of different dinosaurs, and share everything they knew about each. Needless to say, the experts offered more information than the novices. More interesting to Chi and her colleagues was that the experts' responses showed they were thinking about the topic in more complex ways.

The novices stuck to information they could see ("the mouth is open" or "it has three horns") while the young dinosaur experts were more likely to name characteristics that weren't actually depicted in the card ("he is a meat eater" or "they travel in small groups").[30] But the experts also connected the information in a more sophisticated way, making more use of linking words such as *if, because, then,* and *or.* For instance, one child said, "Probably nothing would attack them, *'cause* they're called the King of the Dinosaurs, *so* I imagine nothing could attack them." Another child said, "And *if* they saw a bigger animal, they would run away from it." Responses like this capture far more complex thoughts than the simple chains of description offered by the novices ("He has sharp teeth. He has three fingers. He has sharp fingers, sharp toes, a big tail"). Finally, the experts were able to assign unfamiliar dinosaurs to categories or groups based on some underlying similarity; for instance, one child said, "That can tell me it's a meat eater alright . . . cause it has all these front things around it . . . and that would keep it safe." Chi and her colleagues argued that when children had a lot of information about a domain, it led them to have more integrated and cohesive thoughts—they offered comments that suggested deeper and richer thinking about the topic. Crucially, however, those ways of thinking did not spill over to their thinking about other topics about which they knew little.[31] The study's findings suggest that when children know a lot about something, they reason in more complex ways. So the sophistication of thinking a child can employ is not solely governed by that child's overall developmental level. It is also a function of his or her specific familiarity with a topic.

The findings tell us something about collections, as well. When children collect information, however meandering and sporadic those collections may be, they are not only gathering bits of information but also laying the groundwork for a kind of thinking not otherwise possible. Connecting information, identifying underlying principles, going beyond the obvious to the nonobvious—those kinds of thinking emerge only when one possesses a certain critical mass of information within a domain.

According to this line of thinking, once Addie had collected various kinds of bugs and bug encounters, she could think different kinds of thoughts about bugs. To those who spent time with and around Addie, this certainly seemed to be the case. When Pickle left the slimy piece of ham, crawling with ants, untouched, Addie explained with great authority: "Too many ants for Pickle. They always go like that. They go together. Like a army. Ant Army."

But by Addie's sixth birthday, bugs had been pushed aside. It's not exactly that she turned her attention to something brand new, or discovered a topic she liked better. Rather, bugs were subsumed by something larger—quite a bit larger—though, at first, neither she nor anyone else realized that. One unusually balmy day in April, Addie had gone along for a trip to the supermarket with her babysitter, Margaret. Suddenly the car slowed down, and stopped on the side of the road. Margaret announced, "Let's take a look." Addie, at five and a half, was too low in her seat to spot what Margaret had seen, but trusted it would be interesting. The two of them had already spent an extravagant number of hours exploring outside—in her yard and Margaret's, around the local pond, and in the woods behind the cemetery—finding specimens to touch, smell, and inspect. Once, the year before, Margaret had brought over a sheep's bladder in a jar. It sat on the kitchen table at Addie's house for a week, where the two of them could look and discuss it to their hearts' content. So, when the car abruptly veered over and came to a stop, Addie was ready for action.

Margaret opened Addie's door, unbuckled her, and pointed toward the weedy berm. There lay a very large bird, one wing tip touching the pavement, the rest screened by tall grass. As they approached,

Addie thought it looked as large as she was. It lay in a position she knew was odd. Even though she had never seen such a bird in real life before, she had seen pictures in books. Its neck was long, and curved like the pipe under her kitchen sink. Its body was limp, heavy-looking, and still. She'd seen that look before. It was dead.

"A blue heron!" announced Margaret. "I've never seen a blue heron on the side of the road before. It's so big. I wonder what happened." Then, she strode back to her car to pull out the shears she kept on hand just for opportunities like this one and called out, "Let's see if we can take a leg." Crouching down together in the damp, dirty grit of springtime, they went to work. Addie grabbed the heron by the foot. "Stretch it out," Margaret said, "and I'll cut." The foot was large. Addie needed both hands to straighten out the leg. "Pull," Margaret said. Addie pulled. But she wanted to see close-up as Margaret actually made the cut. She leaned forward, pushing her face near to the heron. "Pew," she said. "Stinky." As the shears bore down on the skinny, scaly leg, she peered even more closely, completely alert. Cutting the leg was not easy. Margaret grunted with effort, and as the blade bit through the leathery skin and bone, Addie heard a grinding crunch. The leg didn't fall away cleanly; Margaret had to pry open her shears and pull it away from the metal. She held it up so they could both look more carefully at the four long talons, each ending in a narrow, hooked toenail. Addie, a chatterbox, had stopped talking. So much to absorb. The skin on the leg was covered in small bumps, an ugly greyish-beige. Where Margaret had cut it, there was a tiny dark tangle of what looked like thin wires. Margaret stood up, holding the sheers, and said, "Okay, you hold onto it, we'll take it to your house." The leg was oddly cool to the touch.

The experience of assisting in her first amputation on that warm and tangy spring day didn't seem like a harbinger. The dead heron encounter came and went like any other number of absorbing moments in the life of a young child. Even though the two of them spent an hour more, back at the house, wrapping string around the leg and tying it up to dry from a far corner of the garage roof, by suppertime Addie had gone to watch her brother play baseball. By the time she was drifting off to sleep, hours later, the heron leg was far from her mind, which was teeming instead with other pressing thoughts. She told her mother all about what she had played with her friends during the baseball game, the scratch on her knee, and what she wanted for her birthday. But the next morning, as she sat at the kitchen table and chewed on a toasted waffle, she caught sight of the tied-up bird leg hanging under the garage, swinging slightly in the breeze. A question struck her and she promptly consulted her brother, age eleven, who seemed to know everything.

"How come there's no blood?"

"No idea," he shrugged. "Ask Margaret."

Hours later, when Margaret met her as she got off of the school bus, Addie wasted no time: "How come there was no blood?" Her curiosity had easily retreated during the day, subsiding to a quiet corner of her mind and making room for the business of school (a spelling test, lunch, kickball, "mad minute" math worksheets, and a girl throwing up at the conclusion of gym class), but as she settled into her seat toward the back of the school bus, thoughts of the leg resurfaced. By the time she saw Margaret through the window, her question had once again become urgent. Addie was lucky. Margaret was the perfect target for Addie's need to know. Margaret didn't ignore Addie's question, but she didn't exactly answer it, either. Instead, she said, "Let's go look at it and see if it's dry enough yet."

"Dry enough for what?" Addie asked.

"To take down and put in your room, so you'll always have it," Margaret answered. Dropping Addie's lunch box and small, torn backpack at the edge of the driveway (both tended to be slobs), they walked

straight over to the bird leg. It had a funny smell. But that didn't stop
them. Margaret grabbed Addie around her stocky legs and hoisted her
straight up, so that Addie could bend slightly and get a good close-
up look.

"Does it look squishy where we cut it, or nice and dry?"

"A little squishy" Addie answered. "Wait, don't put me down yet.
I want to see the blood. Where's the blood?"

"No blood," said Margaret. Addie, not quite believing, peered
closer. "Once it's really nice and dry, you can put it on your book-
shelf and save it forever. Look how cool its toenails are. They're so
shiny and black."

Addie reached out and slid her fingertip along the nail—pressing
the end to see how sharp it was. Then her finger skimmed along the
scaly skin. She couldn't help herself, she also had to pinch the fatter,
wrinkly part halfway up the leg. "Look at his knee, it's all wrinkly and
gobbly, like mom's elbows." Margaret lowered Addie's upright body
to the ground.

"Let's keep our eyes out. Maybe now that it's spring, we'll find a
dead rabbit, and you can add a rabbit skeleton to the collection."

Over the next ten years, Addie's collection expanded. Whenever she
and Margaret detached some part of roadkill or found a small carcass
in a field, they'd scrape it, clean it, soak it in bleach, then hang it outside, until they had a specimen that seemed like it would last. Sometimes they'd look up an animal online or in an Audubon guide to find
out more about how it lived. Other times they'd just poke, prod, study,
and guess how it died.

One summer day when Addie and her family were staying with her
grandparents, she found a dead sand shark on the beach and dragged
it the quarter of a mile back to the house. Her grandmother wouldn't
let her bring it inside, so it was left outside, near a cellar door. By the
next morning the stench was overwhelming—but Addie didn't mind.

She kept sniffing deeply, then making loud sounds of disgust, in equal parts entranced and repulsed. It lay there for days, with Addie returning frequently to inspect it and try to figure out how to add it to her collection. Finally, her older brother, now fifteen and the proud owner of a very sharp folding knife, agreed to help. After transporting the animal far enough from their grandparents' house so that the rest of the family wouldn't have to keep smelling its rotting flesh, he started cutting away to expose the fine, spiky bones, and even more intensely odorous insides. The two of them worked on it for several hours. At one point, as a slab of dense, dark, red meat fell away to reveal skeleton, Addie informed her brother that fish are ectotherms—"not like mammals—not endotherms like rabbits or chipmunks."

By the time Addie was eleven, her zoological collection filled up three walls of her bedroom. By the time she was thirteen, she was not only preserving her own local discoveries but using her allowance to buy more exotic ones. Maxilla & Mandible, the famous (now defunct) emporium in New York City's upper west side, was a favorite store. Relatives who traveled brought her specimens from far away. She had what her uncle assured her was a raccoon's penis bone, a preserved alligator, and eventually a small tortoise. A giant vertebra from a whale was bequeathed to her by an old family friend who had discovered it washed up on an Atlantic coast beach many years before. Once, to her enormous delight, her grandmother took her to visit a friend, a nature writer, who had taken an expedition to the Amazon and somehow acquired a shrunken head. Gawking at it there on the shelf, perched between a dictionary and several of the author's own books, Addie couldn't help imagining the experience of the unfortunate victim. Later she would read about the actual steps in the head-shrinking ritual, but the first vision her mind summoned up was of a tribe's enemy screaming as he or she was flung into a bubbling cauldron, then eventually boiling down to a tiny size. She periodically mused to her mother about how this gruesome scenario might have played out. It bothered her, and she kept right on thinking about it.

The information Addie gathered along the way expanded far beyond the walls of her bedroom. Every time one of her teachers invited students to choose a topic to write about, Addie wrote about animals—where they lived, what they ate, their hunting strategies, who their predators were, how their organs worked, and what their scat looked like. Her knowledge began to organize itself into her own personal Audubon guide. What was, at first, a growing list of facts and observations (herons are birds, bird legs have hardly any flesh on them, fish are ectotherms, rabbits are bloodier than herons) quickly became a body of information too complex to be represented simply as a list. Those specific items she had mentally stored about fish, rabbits, and herons had mushroomed into a vast network of information that offered her not only dynamic clusters of information about a wide range of species, but a hierarchy showing how those species related to one another. Addie was not exceptional in this regard. That kind of layered, structured knowledge is available to any child who is allowed to gather enough information about something she is interested in.

In her pioneering research, set in actual classrooms as well as labs, psychologist Ann Brown showed that when children are allowed to dive into a topic thoroughly, they vastly improve their ability to connect isolated facts in order to generate new ideas. But her research also showed how important it was for students to have agency over what and how they learned, a concept introduced by the cognitive psychologist Jerome Bruner. When Brown and her team invited fourth-graders to dive into the question of how animals create and choose their habitats, they gave the students wide latitude in choosing their subject matter. It was essential, Brown learned, that the kids truly be interested in the set of questions they pursued. This wasn't just a matter of motivating the children, or making it fun. Instead, interest seemed to drive their mastery of information. Equally important, it prompted them to organize the information well enough to teach other students what they had learned, and to come up with novel proposals about animals and their environments.[32]

By the time she was in junior high school, Addie could do more than merely retrieve facts on demand. Given just a few pieces of information about a creature—perhaps it was cold-blooded, furless, and had a certain skeletal shape—she could speculate on its eating habits, its vulnerabilities, and even what kind of nervous system it was likely to have. And she loved to speculate. As her knowledge grew, the ordinary range of animal life she encountered offered fewer and fewer surprises to her. But the same knowledge that dampened the novelty of some of the animal world gave her the capacity to generate new surprises. She guessed what a fly would do if it were left in the freezer for ten minutes and then allowed to warm up again. One summer she repeated her magic trick of bringing the dead back to life to practically everyone who visited her home. She made predictions about which food might lure a chickadee onto her palm. When she and her brother discovered the remains of freshly killed baby rabbits flung against the wire fence bordering their father's garden—the gory aftermath of a lawnmower hitting their nest—she conjectured something about the anatomy of a bunny's eye, then ran inside for a pair of tweezers so she could perform the necessary dissection. With each layer of *actual* new facts, the world of *possible* facts expanded.

Sometimes Addie's interest in the animal world and her love of collecting specimens catapulted her into surprising encounters. One afternoon she was on the lawn swinging a bat, practicing to get good enough to play with her older brother. Out of the corner of her eye, she caught sight of a snake, about a foot long, lying inert on the edge of the grass. She dropped the bat, marched over toward the snake, and crouched down to get a closer look. The snake, evidently dead, had a strange bulge just below its head. She called out to Margaret, who was just inside, watching through the window. "Come out here. Something cool!" Then, when Margaret arrived at her side: "What is it?"

As Addie reached out to stroke the bulge and try to decipher what it was, she noticed something hanging out of the snake's mouth. It was a tiny little frog foot. The foot wiggled. "It's still alive," Addie cried out. "Let's save it!"

Margaret, still a willing partner in taxidermy, walked into the kitchen in her steady, calm way and came back with a paring knife. "You grab the snake body by both ends and stretch it out. I'll cut down the middle so we can rescue little froggy." Margaret said. Addie happily and confidently took both ends of the dead snake and pulled it straight, so that Margaret could slice it open. But as the knife tip entered its flesh, the snake began whipping its head, held in Addie's left hand, back and forth. So the snake was still alive. But with the opening already big enough, Margaret managed to grab the frog between her thumb and forefinger. Now they could see that it was in fact dead. Addie flushed with surprise and dismay. They had gotten it wrong, and now because of them the snake would die, too.

"That's okay" said Margaret. "It happens sometimes. We just made a mistake, that's all. And now you'll have two new things for your shelf."

Young Collectors

Not all children are drawn to such visceral collections. Take William Reese, for instance. By the time he died in 2018 he had become a leading expert on Americana and books on American history—as the *New York Times* obituary described him, a "towering figure among rare book sellers."[33] His interest dated back to his childhood in Maryland, where he was born in 1955. His father loved birds and cherished John James Audubon's paintings of them, and took Reese along on trips to Philadelphia and Baltimore to buy Audubon prints. Even in his youth, Reese preferred spending time with the records and representations of things to spending time with the physical things themselves. "Black Angus cattle were raised on the Reese farm, but William had no desire to be a cattleman himself," the *Times* reported. "Instead, he published his first bibliographic study, *Six Score: The 120 Best Books on the Range Cattle Industry,* while he was still an undergraduate." Years later when he became known as a dealer in old books and prints, he preferred to think of himself as a seller of "evidence." It was the evidence and the provenance of that evidence that captivated him.

For many children who love books, it is not the artifact of the book itself that seems worthy of collection and consideration. It's the contents that enthrall them—the characters, their relationships, and their adventures. Many grownups who take time to reflect on how their intellectual and professional lives were shaped point to particular fiction read when they were young. Francis Spufford, for example, in *The Child that Books Built,* describes the way in which particular books, like *The Wind in the Willows, The Chronicles of Narnia,* and *The Hobbit,* to name just a few, gave him different worlds to think about, and affected the way he navigated his non-reading life. He writes:

> Arthur Ransome's *Swallows and Amazons* series, for example, apart from giving me an enormous crush on Captain Nancy Blackett of the Amazons, always reminded me of my cousins, a large practical family in Cambridgeshire who messed about in canoes on fen rivers just (I thought) like the Ransome children did in sailing boars on Lake Windermere. Idylls of meticulous

detail, instructive about semaphore and surveying and gold re-
fining, the twelve Ransome books let me try out a counterlife
for size: a wonderfully prosaic alternative to my own small,
dreamy, medically unlucky family of four. Here, brothers and
sisters were robust. They milled around. The parents waved the
adventurers off at the dock on page one, and no intense spot-
light of anxiety fell on anyone. The stories blended with the life
I imagined my cousins had. Without having to feel disloyal, I
could experiment, reading Arthur Ransome.[34]

In *My Life in Middlemarch*, Rebecca Mead describes reading George
Eliot's *Middlemarch* for the first time as a seventeen-year-old, immediately sensing that she and the character Dorothea were kindred
spirits, and feeling that "the book was reading me, as I was reading
it."[35] She goes on to describe how her small cluster of friends, living
in a poky English town, shared books and talked about them as a way
to explore life together. One was absorbed by D. H. Lawrence, another by F. Scott Fitzgerald, and she, of course, by Eliot. "Books gave
us a way to shape ourselves—to form our thoughts and to signal to
each other who we were and who we wanted to be. They were a part
of our self-fashioning, no less than our clothes." Mead experienced
herself through the character of Dorothea, but she also learned a
great deal of information from *Middlemarch*. Different kinds of information rose to the surface depending on what was happening to
her. She describes, for instance, giving birth to a son, and suddenly
thinking in a whole new way about Dorothea's sister, Celia, and her
obsession with her baby son, Arthur. Rebecca writes to a friend, "All
these years I've thought I was Dorothea, and now I've turned over-
night into Celia."

In both Spufford's and Mead's cases, it wasn't merely that they read
a lot, but more that the specific books they read shaped their interests,

their thinking, and most importantly, their mental worlds. The specific characters, events, and dramas that avid readers encounter in stories add up to a store of knowledge just as butterflies, shells, and fossils do for their collectors. And, eventually, individual facts get grouped together into useful categories. A rock collection might divide along the lines of shiny versus dull; bones might be from creatures that walk, swim, or fly. In the case of books, someone might set apart all the ones with girl heroines or all the ones containing magic.

In turn, these structures of knowledge enable children to generalize. For instance, a bone collector might note that bird skulls are generally smaller than mammal skulls. A reader of children's literature, that young people everywhere have secrets. The knowledge gathered through collections also allows children to speculate. A dinosaur-related collection might lead a child to speculate that if two particular dinosaurs had fought, the smaller one with sharper teeth would win. The reader of tales set in the past might speculate that people long ago had more exciting lives. Collections of knowledge eventually lead to predictions, as well. Addie might think, about a raccoon head, "if I let this dry it will get a lot smaller." The veteran reader starting on the first Narnia book might predict that, by the end of the story, the children would forget they had ever been through the back of the wardrobe. Finally, these surprisingly large and often intricately organized collections of information allow children to ask new questions: *Do birds carry their eggs inside of them?* or *What happens if the good guy loses?* It's not just that gathering and sorting information on a topic *allows* new questions, it *provokes* them. What were once arresting details (the bones that lie beneath fur and scales, the various shapes of shells, or the inevitable glory that comes from suffering) form a springboard. Driven by their need for novelty, young collectors are catapulted into finding new sources of surprise.

Children all over the world acquire knowledge by gathering objects, listening to stories, and reading books. But some children's collections are quirkier than shells or tales of adventure. I interviewed thirty-six parents about their young children's collections, and asked thirty-two young people about the things they collected as children. One of the latter responded instantly with "I had a collection of fragile things." Laughingly, she said it was made up of "everything that seemed delicate to me, or could break easily. Some things really were fragile, like the shells of baby birds. Other things just looked as if they could be fragile—old pieces of jewelry I found in thrift stores." Another young woman described "an odd assortment" of things she thought of as a collection: "Everything belonged to someone who was dead, or who no longer lived near me."

One nine-year-old boy described to me, in detail, his longtime interest in superheroes. His mental collection of characters included well-known ones (Spider-Man, Green Lantern, the Hulk) and also more than thirty lesser-known characters he had discovered online or in obscure comic books. But he wasn't interested in mastering the details of their profiles, their origin stories, or their most famous adventures. Instead, his whole focus was on learning their fighting styles, understanding their strategies and gauging their relative strengths as adversaries.

According to his parents he had, since the age of three, spent many hours every week, before and after school, when excused from the dinner table, and on weekends, gathering information about the superheroes, then acting out fight sequences that put that information to use. His own account included a memory of being six, and spending an extended period of time concentrating almost exclusively on the characters and fighting in *Star Wars*. He said he liked to mix up their fighting strategies with "my own moves." He continued, "I'd think about being a Jedi. I'd hit the light saber twice, then swoop my leg, grab the bad guy's hand, or throw a web to pull him towards me, then dropkick him."

Though he spent a lot of time alone researching, thinking about, and acting out superheroes and their fighting habits, he also shared this mental world with good friends. "Sometimes I talk with my friend Zach—he loves the DC universe and I pretty much love Marvel universe, and we like talk about 'em like, 'if there were no other universes—just DC and Marvel—DC would crush Marvel. But if there were other universes, like Spider-Verse, then Marvel would win."

These childish lines of inquiry, whether rocks, heroines, or fighting, provide children with a rich resource for thinking new thoughts, asking new questions, and bushwhacking their way into new topics and layers of the world around them. Yet, as noted earlier, not all children's interests are as palpable, sturdy, or easily named as shells or even fragile things. Many of their interests are more fleeting. Sometimes the targets of their curiosity are uncomfortable for them to consider, and equally uncomfortable for adults to acknowledge. My own research on curiosity suggests that, at a surprisingly early age, children are curious about some of the same complex, disturbing, vast, and important questions adults wrestle with—among them immortality, sex, invisibility, God, and the mysteries of technology. One reason we know so little about these more ephemeral and cerebral childhood interests is that it is hard to capture the relevant data. Young children don't easily articulate the more abstract puzzles they're trying to solve, and hints of their interests peak out at unexpected moments. Luckily, we now have more data than ever to help in our quest for answers.

God, Sex, and Other Collections

In 1984, the internet had only existed for a year and the World Wide Web was still years away. But two developmental psychologists, Brian

MacWhinney and Catherine Snow, saw the opportunity to create a valuable online database. It would be a central research repository for diaries parents had kept of their children's language and recordings psychologists had made of children going about their daily lives. They named it the Child Language Data Exchange System, or CHILDES. Some of the data sets available through it date back to the 1960s, and the archive has continued to expand. CHILDES now contains language records in more than twenty-six languages, and includes more than 130 distinct language collections.[36]

Recently, some of my students and I made use of CHILDES data, examining all the collections in which a child pursued a line of inquiry or speculation over multiple exchanges, to find out what kinds of things keep children interested over time. We found that whether they are playing, eating dinner, or riding in the car, children display interest in topics as challenging as the mysteries of technology, justice, invisibility, and death.[37]

In the following two recorded interactions, for example, a four-year-old boy named Abe muses about God. In the first, Abe is chatting with his mother.

Child: Okay. Mommy. Do you remember heaven?
Mother: Uh huh.
Child: I do, too, 'cept I don't remember where it is.
Mother: I thought we decided it was in the sky.
Child: Yeah, 'cept I've never seen it.

A recording three months later of Abe chatting with both of his parents shows his interest in the topic has been sustained.

Child: God's foot is so big, real big.
Mother: You've been thinking a lot about that lately.

Child: Every day.

Father: How big is it, Abe? Bigger than my foot?

Child: Yeah. Bigger (than your foot), than anybody's foot.

Father: What would happen if he stepped on the earth?

Child: God's foot is the earth.

Father: It is the earth?

We don't yet have a full picture of how children collect information about death. But we know more than we did ten years ago. Psychologists and anthropologists, for example, have looked at differences in what children from various cultures hear about the afterlife. Many children in the United States learn from adults that loved ones' spirits go to heaven, where they can continue to see and hear the people they love. Children growing up among the Vezo people, a rural community in Madagascar, learn that spirits from some people who have died will linger among the living and cause trouble. In both cases, the talk children hear about the process of death layers new conceptions of mortality on top of notions they construct through their own observations of people, animals, and plants.[38] What adults say and ask shapes children's thoughts even to the extent of the kinds of thoughts they consider pursuing.

Laura, one of the children whose language was included in the CHILDES database, was recorded on different occasions across five years. Between the ages of four and six, she periodically revisited the subject of death. Take, for example, an exchange she had with her mother and father after her pet bird's death.

Mother: . . . and he got himself ready to die, Laura. He took his nest down and he knew he was dying and he got himself ready.

Laura: He knew he was dying?

Mother: Yes.

Father: He knew.

Laura: How did he know he was dying?

Mother: He could feel inside.

Father: A feeling in the air.

Laura: I don't want to die.

Mother: Mm. We're not going to.

[Laura went on playing on her own, but resumed a few minutes later.]

Laura: I wonder what it feels like to be dead.

In this two-year span, Laura referred to death more than ten times in recorded conversations.[39] This might not sound like a topic of great interest compared to, say, the barrage of references from a child preoccupied by dinosaurs. Nevertheless, it is striking. Occasional comments and queries about death are more likely to fly under the radar, less likely to be identified as a favorite subject than say, chatter about trucks, robots, or fairies. They may lack the charm of such infatuations, but they reflect just as robust an intellectual pursuit, if not more so.

In his early work on imagination, Paul Harris describes a four-year-old boy asking, "It is only the naughty people who are buried, isn't it, because auntie said all the good people went to heaven?"[40] My interviews with parents and recordings of children in their everyday settings suggest that at least a third of children between the ages of three and six ask questions about dying and death, and most of them pursue their inquiries over a period of months or years. These questions are often prompted by a particular event (overhearing news of someone's death, or finding a dead bug or animal nearby) but it appears that, having considered some version of the fact of death, the child wants to know more, and feels (as an adult would) a need to keep revisiting this realm of uncertainty.

Even at four, children are engaged in the difficult work of resolving uncertainty about God and death. There's also the massively mysterious and alluring topic of sex. In the early part of the twentieth century, Susan Isaacs oversaw a children's center, the Malting House School in Cambridge, England. Her observations there of students between the years 1924 and 1927 led to her two classic volumes, *Intellectual Growth in Young Children* (1930) and *Social Development in Young Children* (1933).[41] Among other things, she analyzed the questions individual children asked their parents and teachers over a two-year period between the ages of two and five. Consider two snippets from a diary kept by the mother of a little girl named Ursula, as reproduced in Isaacs's *Social Development in Young Children*.[42] The first records a conversation when Ursula was age three years, nine months:

(3:9) U. was with her mother while she was bathing. Her mother said, *U., do you know what's in here?* "No, what?" *Your little brother or sister.* She went very red and said in a weepy voice, 'Why, Mummy?' I don't want one while I'm little. I don't want one till I'm big." This was repeated several times. Then followed various questions and comments: 'Why do you have it there?' *To keep it warm till it's ready to come out.* When will it come out? Tomorrow? *No, not for a long time, not till the summer.* Why not? *It's not strong enough or big enough yet.* How big is it? *So big, I should think.* Where will it come out? *There.* How will it get out? *When it's big enough and strong enough it'll push and I'll help it until it gets out.* How will you push? *Like this.* How did you make it? Did Daddy plant a seed? *Yes.* When did he? Last night? *No, not then.* When we were on our holiday? *Perhaps.* Was I there? *No, I don't think so.* Was I asleep? *Perhaps.* Why did you make it?

The questions continued in that conversation. And Ursula was still seeking answers in the following month:

(3:10) "Mummy, how did Daddy plant a seed in you?" *It's hard to explain, U. I must think of some way to explain so that you will understand it.* Tell me now, Mummy, how did he? *I promise to tell you later on. I can't until I think of a way to tell you.* I'll ask Daddy. He'll know. *Yes, perhaps he'll be able to explain.* He ought to know. He did it.

And a few days later, Ursula returned again to the matter in question:

How does Daddy plant the seed, Mummy? *Oh, U., I must think of a way to explain it. It's a hard thing to explain.* Yes, but *how,* Mummy, *how?* Where does he keep the seed? *In his underneaths.* Why? *Oh it's a good place to keep it.* How does he plant it? *He just puts it in.* Where?

Ursula's questions are not exceptional. They're typical, and typically overlooked. Nearly every parent can recall a point at which their young children wondered about some aspect of sex. But such curiosity is rarely taken seriously. The common responses of distaste, discomfort, or mild amusement obscure our ability to appreciate the intellectual value of children's pursuit of knowledge, whatever the topic. Moreover, not all children develop the disposition to pursue puzzles that intrigue them. In fact, by the middle of elementary school, many children would be at a loss to tell you what their intellectual preoccupations are.

Are there clues that would help us foster the pursuit of interests in more children more of the time? What lures children to some monumental mysteries, and keeps them engaged?

Making the Familiar Strange

A new line of research has begun to explore the role that awe might play in arousing children's interest. Joseph Colantonio and Elizabeth Bonawitz recently conducted an experiment with ninety-one preschool children in which each was shown one of three short (two-and-a-half minute), emotion-inducing video clips. Some of the children saw a compilation of moments from BBC One's *Walk on the Wild Side*, featuring animals doing funny things, meant to elicit happiness. Others watched a calm segment about small animals in nature. And a third group saw clips from BBC's *Planet Earth*, intended to evoke awe (defined in this context as a sense of wonder, a feeling of being small in comparison to the scale of what one encounters, and a feeling of connectedness to the larger world). Then children were given a chance to play with a complicated and interesting toy—a box that had various knobs and levels which could be turned, yanked, and pulled, plus a magnifying glass that could be looked through, a whistle, and various other engaging features. The box afforded thirty different manipulations. The researchers found that children who had viewed the awe-inspiring clip showed more curiosity in the box. They played with it longer and tried out more of its options.[43] In one suggestive study (wonderfully titled "Oh the Things You Don't Know . . .") Jonathon McPhetres used virtual-reality videos to induce awe in some subjects, while other subjects were offered the same new information, but without the awe-inspiring features. The subjects who felt awe were more aware of what they didn't know about the topic. And when they had completed the activity and were presented with choices to accept as their reward, those who had seen the awe-inspiring version of the video were more likely to choose the free pass to a science museum.[44]

Often the most compelling questions, the ones children seem to mull over again and again, are too complex to grasp or resolve in one exchange. Why wouldn't understanding the daily fall of darkness, or an explanation for rain, much less the details of procreation, or the mystery of God's voice, take some time? It should be no surprise that phenomena such as these might require more than one discussion.

Often children return to a topic again and again because each time they ask a question about it, adults give them vague or partial responses. Research by Chouinard, by Harris, and by Kathleen Corriveau, among others, has shown that when young children get uninformative or unsatisfying answers to their questions, they persist, asking more questions, and posing them in a different way—they are skilled interrogators.[45] But there are other, more satisfying ways than mere vagueness to encourage children's intellectual tenacity.

One way is to offer them interesting mysteries. In one test of this idea, Jerome Rotgans and Henk Schmidt gave ten-year-old students in Singapore the chance to learn more about the physics of light. Twice a week for four weeks the students were provided with intriguing scenarios that provoked them to find out more about why and how light works. (In one session, for instance, the children read a story about a group of friends entering a cave to explore. One of the friends wants to bring a flashlight, but another insists it isn't needed it because their eyes will adjust to the dark). After each session's scenario was presented, the researchers asked the children a series of questions about how much it had stirred their interest. The researchers found that when the children's interest was especially piqued, they developed a more lasting interest in the general topic.[46]

Inherent complexity, unanswered questions, and specific interests are three features that elicit children's sustained curiosity. There is also another one: worry. Children pursue topics that are disturbing. As a source of arousal, worry is good for curiosity but easy to misunderstand—especially when it comes from a child. When I began work on this book, I gave a talk at a small gathering of developmental psychologists.

I speculated that children often want to know about things that are less immediate and concrete than what is under the rock, or why the ball sinks to the bottom of the tub. I suggested that children ponder weightier and more diffuse problems, at least some of the time. During my presentation, a young professor, whom I'll call Janine, tilted her head quizzically and said nothing. She was clearly skeptical about what I was claiming. Later in the afternoon, many hours after my presentation, she pulled me aside. "At first, I couldn't figure out what you were talking about," she said. "It seemed crazy to say that three- and four-year-olds pursue topics over time. I was thinking, 'you're wrong—they want to know about things like why the neighbor's dog barks more loudly than theirs, or what makes the toaster pop up.' But what you said kept tickling my brain." And then, she said, it dawned on her:

> For the last year or so, most nights when I tuck in my four-year-old, Cecile, she asks me questions about dying. I always rush to reassure her that none of us are about to die, that she needn't be scared. Once I've reassured her, I forget about it, figuring I've banished her worry. But it now occurs to me that I've been overlooking what is really going on. She's *interested* in death. It's an intellectual puzzle to her. A troubling one, no doubt. But a puzzle nevertheless. And aren't many of the most interesting ideas slightly troubling?

By the time Addie was fourteen, she knew the names of most insects that lived near her home. She also had a wide and thorough knowledge of animal anatomy. But her eagerness had waned with regard to cutting off legs, skinning, gutting, and drying small animals, and shopping for more exotic specimens in specialty stores. By now, the shelves in her room contained over 130 skulls of all sizes, but they began to collect dust. The objects were no longer of much interest to her. Her attention had turned to something else: the natural history of the animals.

Like so many scientists before her, she found the questions of how and when these species had diverged in form and function endlessly fascinating. To feed her curiosity, she talked to others—her beloved babysitter and her one good science teacher. But soon enough, she craved new kinds of explanation. She had questions that neither the people around her nor her own bone collection could answer. So, she turned to books, beginning with ones written for high school students. But these merely whetted her appetite, and often felt unsatisfying. Their factual information and straightforward explanations barely scratched the surface. The more Addie learned about natural history, the more interested she became, and the more her curiosity extended beyond the information itself to how the scientists did their work. She craved the chance to make scientific discoveries of her own. She began to imagine doing rigorous experiments herself.

In tenth grade, Addie came up with a research question based on her own experience of growing up near a vernal pool and watching caddisflies come to the surface each spring. Was it possible that caddisfly larvae could communicate? She was as curious about what kind of data would answer her question, and how she would collect it, as she was for the answer itself. With permission from her mother to order a large net, she began mapping out the days and hours when she could collect the larva from the vernal pool. She taped sheets of paper to the walls of the basement where she kept the larva, so that she could record their behavior.

At eighteen, Addie went off to college, to study biology.

3

Invention

As a child, I started my own country, which was called Neubern. It was located in the South Atlantic. I did the documentation of Neubern in great detail. I drew everything that was there, all the houses and all the cars and all the people. We even had a navy and an air force.

—Claes Oldenburg

Roger Bolton is old now. His skin drapes over his big frame in baggy folds—slack sails on a ship. His large, brown eyes are somewhat sunken, glowing out from their recessed sockets. He graduated from college in 1959, the year I was born, and received his doctorate from Harvard University when I was in kindergarten. Now an emeritus, he is eminent in the field of economics. He no longer teaches or writes much, but still lives in the college town where he taught for thirty-six years. He shows up every now and then at an academic roundtable or campus lecture that captures his fancy. When Roger speaks, he uses deceptively low-key words and simply constructed sentences. They cloak the rigor of his thinking. He was probably never a show-off, always preferring to communicate his thoughts as if he were talking about the weather, or lunch, rather than mathematical models or principles of economic theory. You might even say that what made his signature piece of work so influential was his skill in marrying so-phisticated economic metrics to people's everyday experiences.

In 1978, when he was in his early forties, Bolton began to develop the work for which he is known, using such well-established tools of economic research as cost-benefit analysis to argue that people's "sense of place"—their affinity for and commitment to where they live—should be understood as a form of "social capital." He was convinced that local initiatives that built a stronger sense of place (perhaps through historic preservation or festival events or enhanced access to appealing natural features) fueled regional economic growth and therefore offered good return on investment. The benefits, Bolton stressed, were not limited to financial returns: "There is also a basic feeling of pleasure at living in a community, or knowing that others live in such a community, that has been created by a combination of social interactions in a particular setting." He also pointed out that sense of place has the characteristics of what economists call a "public good," in that everyone in the area benefits from it whether or not they personally sacrificed any investment to build it.[1]

Bolton's writing on the topic was published toward the end of the great positivist zeitgeist, when the field of economics was consumed by the idea of "hard data." At the time, there was a general preference among scholars, and to a great extent those in business, to focus on the mechanisms of economic systems that could be most readily mea-sured and modeled. Bolton's work stood in stark contrast to the pre-vailing wisdom. He argued that the best use of the quantitative tools of economics was to clarify phenomena that were real and important but inherently more difficult to model because of their supposed in-tangibility. He wanted the numbers to show that a stronger sense of community and cooperation in a particular geographic setting trans-lates to greater well-being and prosperity.

Bolton is a scholars' scholar, having made his contribution by marrying two fields that seemed, until he said otherwise, to have nothing to do with one another: human geography and development economics. He was a trailblazer not only in using economic data to quantify effects that hadn't been measured before, but in focusing on the region—a specific area of land inhabited by a distinct community of people—as his unit of analysis. Highly regarded within his field, he has spent his whole adult life around other academics, working in one ivy league-ish institution after another. Both of his sons have doctorates and are tenured professors, in two of the best colleges in the country. When one encounters Bolton, now in his eighties, it is as clear as day that he has lived most of his life inside his own head. But you would never have guessed that if you had visited him in his childhood home back in the 1940s.

Bolton grew up on a small farm near Harrisburg, Pennsylvania, nestled between Conewego Creek and Little Conewego Creek. "We didn't say *rural* in those days," he tells me. "We lived in the country." In fact, he lived on a dirt road, miles from any town. There were only a few other houses within walking distance. Until he was almost fourteen years old, when his baby sister was born, he was an only child. Roger attended a one-room schoolhouse a couple of miles away from their home. His father made a good living laying industrial water pipes for a company in Harrisburg, "He used to say he was an outdoor plumber." But the family also grew all of their own vegetables and kept chickens, selling the eggs to supplement the household income.

When it rained in south-central Pennsylvania, it rained hard. "The road we lived on wasn't gravel. Just sand and earth. The rain would pour down and turn the road to wet mud. When that happened, I'd usually spend hours playing in the road. There were very few cars that passed by. The road was mine." Drawn to all that inviting, soaked dirt, Roger would dig, pile, fortify, and carve, constructing networks of waterways. First he'd construct a basic set-up—a section of the road often covering more than twelve square feet, with barriers built up on all sides to contain the water, and culverts and alleys within for it to flow. After that he would tinker for hours, rerouting the water by opening new passages in some places and building up little dams in others. He was fascinated by the ways in which each part of his construction affected all the other ones—everything was interconnected and he could change the dynamics of the whole thing by demolishing or creating one barrier. During the summertime when he had hours and hours at his disposal, he'd stay out there all afternoon, going in only for supper. Often he went back out, the sun having not yet set, only to find his waterways dried up or trampled by a neighbor's dog. But the fleeting nature of his systems didn't bother him. He could still see where his streams, gullies, weirs, and locks had been, and think about the next one he would make. Bolton's memories of building in the mud date from the time he was five. Like all children, however, he first began gathering the mental tools needed to invent well before that.

The First Solutions

It's not really until children are about three years old that they start deliberately identifying problems and constructing solutions to those problems. Their first inventions are unlike the ones that will follow in the years to come. Learning to invent takes time, and the necessary elements don't come together easily. It is not as if the young Roger Bolton played in the mud outside his house, and simply emerged thirty years later capable of producing bold new economic theory. Unlike inquiry, which begins during the first weeks of life, and travels along a pretty steady route, there are several twists and turns on the path to invention. We tend to think children simply get better at important skills as they get older. That is not the case with invention. The process is more circuitous than that.

The three-year-old inventor has some striking limitations in her ability to innovate and solve problems, but she also has some formidable powers the five-year-old does not. What's more, by the time children have acquired the full intellectual toolkit needed to be good inventors, they have often all but lost the will to do so. The path that connects the playful, quirky, and unimportant inventions of early childhood to the profound, complex, and pathbreaking inventions some adults produce is perilous. It's possible for children in early adolescence to be more innovative than they were as preschoolers. But most become less so. The toddler's solutions and fabrications are so abundant that they are fairly invisible to most adults. Yet, however unremarkable they might seem, they set the stage for all the inventions that may lie ahead. The trials and tribulations of the youngest inventors offer clues to how we might encourage children to continue inventing as they grow up.

Imagine the following scene, one that has unfolded in countless homes in towns and cities all around the world. A five-year-old wanders on her own into the family kitchen. She sees the cookie jar up on a shelf, above the counter. She knows there are delicious cookies just waiting for her inside that jar. Of course, she wants one. But she accurately judges that it's too high up for her to reach on her own. What can she do to make the cookie jar reachable? In that moment, as she holds in her mind a tangible goal (getting the cookie), a clear obstacle (the height of the counter), and something halfway between a feeling and a thought (call it a hunch) that maybe she can figure out how to overcome the obstacle, she has her first glimmer of defining a solvable problem. She grabs the seat cushion from a nearby armchair and hauls it over to the counter. She lays it on the floor just below the cookie jar, and steps onto it. She's a little closer to reaching the jar, but her arm still doesn't extend high enough. Again, she has a sense that if she does something more, the problem may yet be solved. She looks behind her and considers the cushion on the back of the chair. She heads over to get it, planning to put it on top of the first pillow. She is on her way to an invention—a plush step stool.

The problem is as old as sweets and high shelves, and the solution she comes up with is just as familiar. There is nothing special or precocious about what she is doing. The sequence unfolds in less than sixty seconds: she casts her frustrations as an obstacle to be overcome; zeroes in on what's preventing her (thereby identifying a problem—a crucial step); scouts around for the gestures and objects that might help her; and puts them together in a sequence and arrangement she hasn't yet mastered or been taught. This combination of analysis and synthesis leads her to a solution she has never before employed. There's nothing truly innovative about piling up objects and climbing on them to grab something you want that's just out of reach. But it's new to her, and that is key.

When it comes to understanding how children's concoctions and constructions lay the foundation for their ideas, it doesn't really matter if an invention warrants a patent. What matters is the psychological process of collecting familiar elements (whether those elements are information or objects) and putting them together in new ways, to solve a problem that matters to the inventor. Consider a second example, just as prosaic and unremarkable as reaching a cookie jar. A four-year-old boy playing in his tub has been scooping up water with a pail and pouring it back into the bathwater. He notices that the empty pail stays afloat. He reaches in to press it down, and it dips, only to bob back up. He pushes it till it touches the bottom of the tub, but the moment he takes his hand away, there it goes, popping right back up to the surface. This is the first psychological moment in the process of invention—his surprise that it doesn't do what some other objects have done before: sink to the bottom.

At this point he might investigate, peering into the pail, or studying the surface of its outside for anything that explains its failure to sink. But his investigations won't only be to get information. He is not just trying to explain the unexpected; understanding why it stays afloat is not, at this moment, his aim. What he has in mind is a submarine. How can he play submarine if this bucket won't stay at the bottom of the tub? What does he need to do to keep it down there? He has a goal beyond information or insight—he wants to enact a specific scenario. To play the game he has in mind, he must figure out how to make the pail stay down. He has now launched himself onto the path of invention. He tries holding it down for ten seconds. That doesn't work. He tries turning it over. Again, no joy. Finally, he grabs some bottles of bubble bath that are standing on the corner of the tub, and a large bar of soap. He puts them inside the pail. It sinks. Along the way, he may have picked up a clue about density. More significantly, he has solved his pressing problem. He has invented his first submarine.

The earliest inventions often appear, to adult eyes, to be simple and obvious (especially when the invention replicates a familiar object— piled cushions become a step stool or heavy objects serve as an anchor). But the psychological steps involved in even those rudimentary and well-worn solutions to simple problems require a complex set of intellectual moves that include identifying the contours of the problem, feeling that one can deliberately try things to solve the problem, imagining a solution, and envisioning the steps one might take to reach that solution. Consider the little boy in the bath. He has to imagine the pail as a submarine prowling at the bottom of the tub before he can try figuring out what he needs to do to make it happen. But he doesn't have an understanding of the role weight plays in making things sink or float. When he tries pushing it down, he's using a strategy that has worked for him before with other objects in different circumstances. When it doesn't work, he has to be able to generate other options. In this case, prior experience has taught him that heavy things don't float. The first signs of flexible thinking about alternative solutions is already apparent, right there in the bathtub.

Babies employ a small but powerful repertoire of actions to interact with their worlds. The repertoire begins with reflexes like sucking and noticing the unexpected. These seemingly humble behaviors set them on their way toward thinking. Yet, even though their bodies and minds are extraordinarily active, babies and toddlers are not yet innovative and they aren't deliberate problem-solvers. Over the next several years, almost all of them will acquire a complex portfolio of knowledge and intellectual skills that will enable them to invent. But those components don't emerge in a neat, linear sequence.

Preschoolers have a grasp of some steps but find others elusive. Over the next three or four years, however, everything will change. By the time they are eight, the intellectual repertoire of young inventors is nearly complete. The scientific story of how children get to be better inventors is not straightforward, and it's filled with paradox. The story begins with hammers and knives.

Old Tools, New Tools

Human beings have achieved their dominance on this planet in part through their extraordinary capacity to use tools. We have fashioned arrows to defend ourselves and conquer others, knives to harvest and hunt, wheels and steam engines to travel and transport, and lenses to boost our limited vision. As far back as 100 BCE, Greeks invented something called the Antikythera mechanism—the first version of a computer, made of over thirty meshed bronze gears, which predicted positions of planets and stars, and phases of the moon. It was an extraordinary feat of engineering, and shows that our interest in tools that extend our mental capability is ancient. The use of tools defines human history, and accounts for many of our greatest and most horrifying achievements. We have even invented tools to investigate and record our tool use. This explains the vast scholarly literature on the evolution and history of tool use dating back more than two million years. Those records show that while the inventions themselves have changed, often capitalizing on inventions of a previous era, the underlying psychological processes have not.

All people, whether living in the thirteenth century or the twenty-first, have employed the same basic steps as they piece their way toward new equipment and devices. Fashioning a wheel, crane, or computer takes sophistication, expertise, time, and prolonged effort. Only some of us would even attempt to create such important and complex tools. But the underlying steps are available to almost everyone, and are practiced by nearly everyone, at a very young age, long before any kind of formal education. Children stumble upon the process quite naturally. In fact, using tools is child's play.

Cora was four. She was stocky, with a square jaw and thick brown hair. She spent a lot of time in the yard in front of her house, amusing herself in the hot sun. She had been watching some very small lizards climb in and out of the large rocks just outside her kitchen door. Some of that time she pretended the lizards were dragons, narrating action scenes in which the dragons were hunting and being hunted. Every once in a while, she roared on their behalf. At some point, though, she tired of pretending the lizards were dragons. She began simply watching them. Then she decided she wanted to catch one. The goal of capture riveted her. But it presented a challenge. What would it take to grab a lizard? She started with the best implement of all—her small, pudgy hands. But she wasn't quick enough, and after several tries, she figured out that each time she got too close, the lizard skittered away.

Cora could tell that she needed something more than her hands to catch a lizard. She needed a tool. She looked around and spied a four-inch stick lying in the dirt. The next time the lizard peeked out, Cora quickly pushed the stick toward the lizard. But the stick couldn't catch the lizard any more than her hand could. What's more, the stick she'd grabbed was too short to provide the necessary distance between herself and her prey. She looked around and found a longer stick. Next time a lizard ventured out, she crouched at the end of the path, striking out at the last possible moment. This time the length was good, and she tapped the lizard on its tail. But then it darted away, dinged, but free. She tried it again. She tried it five times. She was what the researchers call *perseverative,* trying the same ineffective method over and over, unclear about what was wrong, or what further steps were called for.

She knew she had to find a way to grasp the lizard from a greater distance. But the tool she had found wasn't adequate. She sat there looking stumped. She didn't know what to do next. Any adult watching would have instantly seen what the problem was, as well as the possible solutions. Cora needed something long enough to reach the lizard, but it would have to include something to trap rather than poke the lizard. But Cora, at four, had hit an intellectual obstacle she couldn't quite overcome.

By the time children have reached their third year, they are eager to use tools and do so quite easily. Take, for instance, the ability of nearly any toddler to learn to drink from a cup or manage a spoon. Surrounded by siblings, peers, and adults who use objects they have never seen before, very young children readily catch on. Copying older people is one of the most effective learning strategies young children possess. Not only does it allow them to quickly absorb valuable techniques, it ensures they will use the particular skills valued by people in their very own community. But learning how to use a tool is not enough. We humans have gotten where we are not only because we *use* tools, but more importantly, because we know how to *devise* new ones. Could Cora come up with the tool she needed, and catch her lizard?

What's the Problem?

If you watch children navigate their everyday worlds, they seem quite resourceful. Some version of reaching the cookie jar is a familiar scenario in every home. Part of their ingenuity comes from their capacity to transform objects, which they constantly do while playing. Using one object to stand in for another is one of the most important first steps toward representing the world in one's mind—a key feature of sophisticated thinking. Three-year-olds who turn a wooden spoon into an airplane, a twig into a magic wand, or a sweater into long, flowing hair are all taking steps toward seeing the world as it could be, not simply as it is. These behaviors are so ubiquitous one rarely notices them, unless one is looking for signs of invention. Recently I observed a four-year-old boy watch his mother lay her oven mitts on the kitchen table after taking a casserole out of the oven. Wasting no time, he marched over to the table and grabbed the mitts. He sat down on the kitchen floor and promptly fitted one onto each of his two feet, lifted them up in the air, and waved them about. "Look, I'm a monkey!" he called out to his twin sister, who was standing nearby. "Look at my monkey feet!" Two-minute transformations like this soon lead to more sustained play. And when children play, they constantly come across problems they must solve.

Consider the following example of three cousins who spent several days a week playing together over the course of their fourth summer. This particular enterprise ended up consuming a great deal of their time and energy. One of the cousins, Nate, lived in a house whose yard bordered some woods. Along the edge of the woods lay several fallen trees, in various stages of rotting, some with their roots sticking high in the air—just the kind of sight that might interest a child. In amongst the fallen trees were also lots of large rocks and boulders, several of them taller than Nate and his cousins. One of the boulders was wide at the bottom and rose out of the ground at least six feet, looming over the children. When they gathered to play, they frequently gravitated to that edge of the property, within eyesight of their parents but on the edge of something wilder and more unfamiliar. On their fourth visit out there, one of Nate's cousins, Lex, said, "See it? See it? It's huge. I know what we can do. It can be the cave."

Both of the other children seemed to know what Lex meant by "the cave." They dragged some fallen branches over and hoisted each one up to the top of the giant boulder, then placed the limb's other end on one of the smaller boulders nearby. A roof began to take shape. During the first weeks of the summer the cave was never far from their thoughts. "Let's go work on the cave," one would say. Or: "It's raining. It's gonna break the roof." They cared about it: "You're messy. Pick up that twig. We have to make sure the cave is neat." And often they talked about the project from the perspective of builders: "That'll be the window." Nate's father was, in fact, a carpenter, and Nate often seemed to be imitating what he had seen his father do and say. As they worked on the roof of their cave, Nate insisted that the branches had to fit together tightly so the rain couldn't get in. The others willingly labored, piling on more and more twigs and branches. As they worked on this part of it, Nate periodically said, "Gotta be airtight." Every once in a while, he'd hold his face very close up to the inside of the roof, and squint to see if light was shining through.

As the three cousins worked, they also chatted about other things (toys, movies, candy, and which of them was the fastest runner). Then, in early July, when they had been working on their cave for several weeks, one of them said, "Hey. We could live in there. Baby animals!" "Yeah," the other two agreed enthusiastically. "Baby animals!" And with that suggestion, the three were launched into a new phase of their game, one they had clearly played before. The particular animals changed from one day to the next. Nate was sometimes a baby raccoon and other days a baby dog, which they referred to as "baby puppy." Lex was often a baby wolf, and the third cousin, Paul, a baby lion or another baby puppy. Using high voices, they'd talk to one another in a form of baby talk, and enact a range of scenarios: fighting, helping one another, seeking food, getting hurt or sick, and periodically worrying out loud to one another about where the mommy and daddy animals had gone.

The children's narration and their actions influenced one another—a phenomenon well-documented in research.[2] At times the language preceded and planned the action: "Let's put the strong branches over here. Yeah, that one there. Get it. It can reach from here to your rock." At other times, their talk changed the play in progress, often adding a symbolic or transformative element to what might otherwise have been a straightforward construction project, "This is where we sleep. It's over here, where it can't get wet. But just say— you just say, 'Baby Raccoon, I'm cold!' And I'll bring you the blanket." And sometimes their language reflected on what had been done. "This isn't working. The sticks are too weak. They're too skinny. We need to make a bridge between the houses. We havta make the bridge strong." The two-way dynamic between actions and words is an early manifestation of children's proclivity to turn the actual into the possible.

Over the course of the summer, the emphasis of the trio's play shifted from making a cave to playing within it. The goals of their play unfolded over time: creating a roof, turning the sides of the boulder into walls, and becoming baby animals. Along the way, each new goal presented problems they needed to overcome. The first goal was how to do something fun with the boulder and the fallen branches. Soon the goal became building a good cave. In turn, that goal led them to make their cave a satisfying setting for their beloved game of "baby animals." Meeting these goals put specific obstacles in their path. How could they strengthen the roof? Could there be bedrooms? How could the baby animals get in and out of the cave? The particulars of that long summer of baby animals and shelter-building were unique to those three cousins. But whenever children play, they stumble across problems which demand solutions. In some cases, the central problem is to invent a new world.

Two six-year-old girls, Maude and Sophie, regularly carpooled to school together over the course of three years. As they traveled back and forth, day after day, Maude and Sophie sat in the trunk seat of Maude's mother's car, facing backwards, where they felt alone, unaware that anyone could see or hear them. During the twenty-five minute drive they chattered nonstop, discussing one thing: an imaginary world they had concocted, which they called Bugzeeland. They endlessly discussed and decided on matters concerning the topography of their new land, the features of the landscape, the characters who lived there, and the languages spoken.

The girls agreed early on that Bugzeeland was a round planet, but that all life on it, instead of existing out on the surface, lived down inside. To get into or out of Bugzeeland, one had to go through a trapdoor.

Characters who lived in Bugzeeland included the Beach Lady, who was very large and sat in her bathing suit on a beach, surrounded by beach umbrellas; the Magician, who guarded a well at the end of the only straight road in Bugzeeland; the Popcorn Piglets, whom the girls kept referring to as "very normal," saying at times that the piglets were so normal they were boring; the two Gods of Bugzeeland, who sat on the sun's rays at the top of the sphere and watered the planet with watering cans; and some other nameless creatures who stood by the trapdoor shoveling dust out of the planet, which then turned into stars in outer space. They also periodically named other characters, but did not develop them as fully: the 41sler, the Firegobbler, the Singer Servants, and the Curly Mold Foot Walker. Other places in Bugzeeland included the City of Toe, which they repeatedly affirmed was shaped like a big toe—the nail being a lake—and a neighborhood shaped like a muffin.

Maude and Sophie spent weeks and weeks inventing the languages of Bugzeeland. They wrote these down in small notebooks brought along in their book bags just for this purpose. They based the languages on the English alphabet, using its sounds and letters, and in one language, repurposed whole words. In the language they called "O.F.," each letter of the alphabet was assigned a different letter (in place of A, B, C, and D, for example, there were O, F, P, and G), making it a kind of code. In the "Zig Zag Manicure" language, it was the same kind of code but using symbols. And a further variation was used in the "And Why" language; here, each letter was replaced with a short word (so that A, B, C, D, E, F, G became And, Why, All, Sky, Are, Star, Dull). The first four languages they created required memorization to be used, so the girls decided to create a fifth, more user-friendly one. This one, which they continued to use throughout middle school, they called Bugzeelish.

Sophie and Maude were absorbed in designing every feature of their imaginary land, and less interested than other children might be in enacting scenarios within it. They took great pains to work out all sorts of details. In cases like this one, it's not that children's play presents them with obstacles to be solved—instead, Maude and Sophie outlined a problem for themselves. What would a completely different world look like and what would be in it? The problem they had set themselves, inventing a new world, captivated them across three years of playtime.[3] Like so many children who create forts, games, and imaginary lands, they were tireless and creative problem-solvers. However, they were not yet using all the methods more experienced inventors employ. Some forms of invention remain stubbornly elusive to the four-year-old.

Other People's Problems

When researchers have tried to examine children's innovations under more controlled circumstances, the picture has looked somewhat different. Asked to devise a specific tool to solve a particular problem, young children often seem stymied. What keeps three- and four-year-old children from devising tools when the ones they find around them won't do the job? In an ingenious series of studies, Ian Apperly, Sarah Beck, and their colleagues tried to identify just why it is that very young children seem to have such trouble contriving a simple tool. They showed individual children between the ages of three and six a clear, plastic, vertically mounted tube, too narrow to reach down into, with a little, handled pail at the bottom, in which an attractive sticker lay. "If you can get the sticker out of that little pail," they told each child, "you can keep it."[4]

Lying next to the tube with the sticker was an array of materials the children could use to devise a way of reaching the sticker. Among the materials was a pipe cleaner. Virtually all of the children seemed keen on getting the sticker, but while the older ones tended to succeed, the three- and four-year-olds could not manage it. Consistently, they were unable to hit upon the obvious (and only possible) solution of choosing the pipe cleaner, bending one end of it into a hook, dipping it into the tube, and pulling up the pail with the sticker. Was it simply that three- and four-year-olds lack the necessary motor skills for this delicate task? No, when they were shown how to do it, they successfully copied the steps (an important skill in and of itself, to which we return later). The researchers considered the possibility that the solution was a bit too complicated. To test that, they set up a similar experiment with a simpler solution. All the children had to do was unbend a pipe cleaner and slip it into the tube, now presented horizontally, to push the sticker out the other end. But making the mechanics of innovation easier did not seem to help the children at all. Perhaps, the researchers thought, the younger children didn't feel as free to fiddle with the materials without explicit permission. To test that, the researchers introduced a puppet named Heinz who offered the materials, saying, "Heinz has some things that you might make into something that could get the sticker." But even offering such a clear and child-friendly prompt didn't have any real impact. Three- and four-year-olds remained unable to fashion a tool while five- and six-year-olds readily did so.[5]

What changes between those ages? Apperly and Beck believe that the younger children are regularly stumped by what is known as an "ill-structured" task—a problem whose specific parameters are not clear to them. They want the sticker, but aren't sure what obstacles they have to overcome. This was a problem Cora faced in her lizard-catching quest. When Apperly and Beck finally showed children two different ways to get the sticker, and asked them to choose the better way, they did fine. And the same would probably have been true of Cora: if someone had shown her two options, a plain stick versus, say, a broom and big cardboard box to knock the lizard down into, she would have chosen the latter. It's not that Cora couldn't have recognized a better solution, but rather that, on her own, she could not think through what capturing the lizard required. She hadn't quite figured out all the contours of the challenge she had set herself.

When I first began looking at the scientific data on children's innovation, something seemed askew. The experiments are unusually ingenious, providing wonderful examples of how an activity designed by a scientist can elicit behaviors that offer a glimpse inside children's minds. But I noticed a mismatch between the laboratory results and my everyday experience. By now, I have been observing preschoolers in action for forty years. I have watched many children in labs, but at least as many on playgrounds, in day care centers, and in the unruly privacy of my own home. The children presented with the sticker in the tube seem more confounded than any child I have ever watched make a trap, build a fort, or fashion a new toy.

I decided to probe the topic a little further with some of my students. We began to think there were two possible ways in which the experiment might not capture the whole story. One of these was a bit elusive, the other quite straightforward, Consider the elusive problem first.

Perhaps expecting children to turn a pipe cleaner into a hook was asking for something too far out of their bailiwick. Perhaps subjects living near or in university towns had little experience with activities that might have prepared them for inventing a hook (going fishing, for instance). Maybe they didn't have the requisite knowledge, and maybe knowledge itself is key to invention.

Does Knowledge Help People Invent?

Filmmakers and journalists love to tell stories about people who hit upon an important invention by accident, or in a flash of creativity. In popular narratives of clever discoveries, the fresh, ingenious idea seems to appear out of the blue. Louis Pasteur notices a strange growth on some liquid accidently left in the lab over a holiday. Ben Franklin uses a kite to detect electricity in a lightning storm. The same is true when lesser-known inventors make their breakthroughs. Bette Graham was a secretary in the 1950s. While rushing to please her boss, she used white tempera paint to hide her typos, and ended up a multimillionaire, having created Liquid Paper.[6] In many of these stories, the inventor is, if anything, helped by a dose of naivete or ignorance. But a close inspection of inventions (the high-impact kind, but also the minor inventions people devise in their everyday lives), shows something very different. Most of these come not from out of the blue, but from familiarity with the domain and plenty of specific information.

My stepfather, a farmer, rarely got through a day without having to figure out a way to keep a pasture gate closed, replace a part on the tractor, or hold in some runaway chicks when he had run out of fine-meshed fencing. His inventions weren't important to the world, but they were useful to him, and often ingenious. His locks, traps, and jury-rigged watering mechanisms emerged from a long history of devising other, similar things. He knew a lot about the materials at hand and a lot, too, about the particular kinds of problems he was trying to solve. Truck drivers are more likely to come up with better ways of securing objects, chefs more likely to work around the absence of certain ingredients, and EMTs more likely to see how to stabilize patients when the usual medical equipment is unavailable. The same is true, needless to say, of less tangible problems. Teachers are more likely to come up with better methods for getting to know a new student and trial lawyers are more likely to think of the best way to get information out of an unwilling informant. Experts are often more inventive than novices.

Perhaps a lack of relevant knowledge, rather than immature cognition, was holding back the children in those studies. Maybe most preschoolers simply haven't had enough exposure to the components required to retrieve an object by making a hook. To investigate this possibility, my student Danielle Faulkner and I invited two groups of children—a younger group of four- and five-year-olds and an older group of six- and seven-year-olds to solve the "retrieve something out of the tube" task, but we added a few wrinkles to it. First of all, instead of a sticker lying in a basket, which seemed like a tepid motivator at best, we built a little guy of brightly colored Play-Doh, and told the children he needed to be rescued from the bottle. Second, before showing the children the bottle with the trapped little guy, we gave some of them knowledge that might help them with the problem. In this way, we could test the hunch that insufficient knowledge, rather than some underdeveloped innovation skill, had been the stumbling block for the younger children studied by Apperly and Beck.

Not all the children who got background information received it in the same way. In one condition, young subjects were read a picture book about a little girl who sees a fish jumping in a pond. She wants a closer look at it, and decides to try and catch the fish. Looking around, she finds a stick, which she bends into the shape of a hook. The story ends with her catching the fish on the hook (whereupon she says hello to the fish and then lets it jump back into the pond). We wanted to know if our young subjects could absorb the information available in that story and then apply it to the pipe cleaner task.

But hearing a story is only one means of becoming more knowledgeable; children also learn through various kinds of firsthand experience.

In a second condition, the experimenter and the subjects tried out different ways to "become a hook" with their own bodies. In a third condition, children watched the experimenter make a hook out of a straw, and use it to pull something through an opening cut in the bottom of a clear plastic bottle. In a fourth condition, children were invited and given plenty of time to play around with the materials (including the all-important pipe cleaner). All of these were variations on equipping the children with relevant knowledge and familiarity with an activity before presenting them with the puzzle of rescuing the little man in the clear plastic bottle. Would that help the children innovate? What we learned was not straightforward.

The older children did very well, quickly and easily bending the pipe cleaner into a hook and using it to rescue the little guy. It didn't matter to this group's results whether they had heard the story, made themselves into a hook, watched an experimenter solve a similar problem, fiddled around with materials, or received no background knowledge at all. The problem and its solution did not appear to require much innovation or puzzling at all. In fact, most of the older children solved the task in less than two minutes.

The younger children, on the other hand, rarely succeeded, even when they had prior access to useful information. None of the conditions meaningfully changed that outcome. At first blush, our data disconfirmed the hypothesis that lack of relevant knowledge was a decisive obstacle getting in the way of young children's innovation. When we took a closer look at what happened during the sessions, however, we discovered something new.

For the kids who solved the problem quickly, it was easy enough to know when the session was over. This was true of almost all the older children in our study. But, again, the problem seemed trivially easy for them, as though they weren't inventing at all, but just applying obvious techniques to an obvious problem. It was the children who didn't solve the problem within two minutes that proved a treasure trove of information. They typically kept trying for several minutes more and tested a variety of approaches. After two minutes, we offered children who had not quickly succeeded some hints, beginning with the very minimal, "Remember what you did before?" To those who still couldn't devise a solution, we ended with "How about making a hook?" This final suggestion worked for all. Watching what they did between initial failure and an eventual (guided) success was one of the most enlightening parts of the study.[7]

Crawling toward Innovation

Often the children tried to get to the guy by using the string or pipe cleaner to poke or slap the side of the bottle. Some children seemed to realize that the hole at the top of the bottle offered a path to success. They'd grab the pipe cleaner (they always chose that first) and would drop it down the opening.

Sometimes, they'd just stab at the small figure. Some children would try to guide the pipe cleaner into the loop made by the figure's arms, without bending it. If they succeeded at placing the end of the pipe cleaner within the loop, the children would vocalize happily and attempt to hoist the figure up, expecting their maneuver to do the trick. But the pipe cleaner was not rigid or strong enough to work. Even when they had it through his arms, raising him only slightly would cause him to slide off. Often, after this technique had failed several times in a row, the children switched strategies or materials. They didn't seem to realize how close they were to success, or think how to tweak their current method. A few children dropped the string inside of the tube, trying to touch the figure and even attempting to thread the string through the loop. Sometimes these same kids would dangle the string into the tube and then pause, as if waiting for the string to exert some causal property independent of them.

The children frequently talked while they were trying to solve the problem. Their comments suggested they were trying to connect what they had heard or done in the first part of the study to the hook task. One child who had heard the fishing story said, when looking at the figure, "It looks like he's a fish." A child who had used his body to make hook shapes asked about the looped arms, "Why does he has a hook thing on top of his head?" One child in the modeling condition, who had watched the experimenter create a hook from a straw in order to pull on a string loop, said, when looking at the guy in the bottle, "This [bendy straw] is like a hook, like the tip, and his arms are like the string." Another said, about his own efforts, "'Cause I saw *this* [pipe cleaner] as a hook and *this* [figure] as a hook." Many of the kids who had heard the story used fishing language as they tried to solve the problem. One asked, "Can I lure him back in?" Another explained that "you had to get it out with a kind of hook shape . . . I was thinking about fishing." Another little boy made it clear that his attempts to succeed were colored by the story he'd heard: "I just need to hook him on. How can you pull this guy up? Wait, let me try something—let me try to do a hook so I can hook it. I need the hook. Let's get the hook out. I'm gonna fish him good!" What children did and said as they struggled with the problem showed that, although they might not have all the components assembled yet in their minds, they were feeling their way, element by element, toward a solution.

Our observations convinced us that researchers should not view innovation as an all-or-nothing achievement. Many subjects in our study who failed to retrieve the figure nevertheless tried techniques that were perfectly feasible. The techniques might even have succeeded with one or two further modifications. By recording what they said, while they fumbled around, we learned that when it comes to devising a specific tool to solve a specific problem, the transition from inability to success is a crawl, not a leap.

We also learned a lot from listening to what the successful innovators said about their mental process as they worked. They seemed aware that they had drawn on specific kinds of knowledge to help them. When asked at the end, "How did you know how to do that?," a child who had watched the experimenter bend a straw to extract something said, "I saw the straw had a hook, so that's how." A child from the story condition said, "I bended the end of the pipe cleaner because in the book she bent it." Another reported that, at first, she "forgot" that a pipe cleaner could bend, but then "I was kind of thinking of the book, how she made it." Finally, one child who had made hooks with her body got to the heart of the inventive process: "It gave me ideas . . . I was bending." We saw children who succeeded easily, and children who never succeeded, all trying to draw on helpful sources of insight.

Like adults, children do their best inventing when they have some prior knowledge and experience in the relevant domain. The children who succeeded quickly and the ones who got partway there drew on their store of information. This helps explain why children seem more inventive when they play than when they are asked to solve an experimenter's task. The problems they solve in play are more meaningful and motivating to them—but also, when they are playing they are more likely to interact with materials and scenarios with which they are familiar. This observation seems so obvious as to be banal. And yet it's routinely overlooked by experiments (and to a degree, by educators).

In the 2015 film *The Martian* (based on Andy Weir's novel of the same name), Matt Damon's character is a botanist who finds himself stranded alone on Mars. Needing to save himself by, among other things, figuring out how to grow food there, he announces to his video diary, "I'm going to science the shit out of this." In its own goofy way, that scene brings to life a key truth. The fuller your intellectual framework for a domain (biology, in this case) the less specific knowledge and familiarity you need (with, say, agriculture on Mars), and the more you can invent solutions based on general principles of how things work. The marooned Mark Watney can innovate because he has so much background knowledge.

Four-year-olds are more likely to have expertise at the things they play regularly, whether mermaid scenarios or airplane hangars. And individual differences rule—one likes mud, another small machine parts. One loves pretend fishing and another loves to play tea party. But culture also exerts a strong influence—nudging children toward some materials and practices, and away from others. Invention, like almost every other emerging psychological process, bears the stamp of a child's community.

To test the importance of community influence, Karri Neldner and her colleagues tried the hook task with children in a wide range of cultures. In addition to testing children from the westernized city of Brisbane, Australia, they tested children from the Ni-Vanuatu communities on the island of Tanna (in the southwestern Pacific Ocean) as well as Kalahari Bushmen children in Platfontein and the Kgalagadi region of South Africa. They also tweaked the method in a few other ways. They gave each child several different kinds of materials, allowed more time with those materials, and recorded what the children did in the time leading up to and after the target behavior. Widening the lens in terms of both culture and the experiment itself turned out to be quite fruitful. Again, the older children in all three cultures proved more efficient and skilled than younger children, but under these revised conditions the younger children succeeded to a greater degree than in previous studies. The children who didn't solve the problem efficiently, completely, or according to the researchers' expectations did tend to try out a variety of techniques in their attempts. For instance, children in non-western cultures sometimes chose three small pieces and shoved them into the tube without connecting them. It worked to dislodge the desired object, even though it wasn't the solution the experimenters had in mind.[8]

Neldner and her colleagues concluded that specific activities and materials within a culture play a big part in nudging children toward one form of innovation over another. But by what means would this transmission work? Fortunately, the mechanism by which specific aspects of culture "get into" children and shape their thoughts and practices has been known for some time.

Ninety years ago, Lev Vygotsky argued that what children can do with help at one point predicts what they will soon be able to do on their own. He called the distance between their current unassisted and assisted capability the "zone of proximal development."[9] Many studies since have shown that the nature of the help involved shapes the child's future intellectual processes. If adults help by suggesting tools, children are subsequently more likely to use tools when doing things on their own. If adults suggest children imagine solutions, that too will become part of their repertoire. Four-year-olds in our lab never solved the hook task without some hints, whether they heard a story about fishing, or acted out various kinds of hooks with their own bodies. Five-year-olds did much better when they were given subtle hints and reminders. Six-year-olds found it so easy they could solve the task with or without any prompts. It should come as no surprise that new ways of thinking and operating in the world emerge with help. There is a psychological bridge that connects the complete inability to do something with the ability to do it easily. That bridge is forged by what children see others do, but also by the specific kinds of assistance they get.

In a captivating study of cultural factors influencing invention, Alex Bell, Raj Chetty, and their colleagues compared the backgrounds of

1.2 million people in the United States who had received patents, with non-inventors who were matched on various characteristics such as socioeconomic status, childhood hometown, and gender. They found that the likelihood of inventing was much higher for children who grew up with more money and various other kinds of class privilege. But beyond those patterns, they found that neighborhoods known for innovation and science contained many more children who grew up to invent, regardless of whether those children had parents who were inventors. Evidently, something about living in a town where invention is valued rubbed off on many of the youngest citizens. One final detail of their results concerns gender. Overall, male children were more likely to grow up to apply for patents. But the gap shrank for girls who grew up in towns with greater numbers of women inventors. Finally, those who grew up to invent tended to apply for patents in the same field of technology that predominated in their childhood neighborhoods. In sum, money wasn't everything. And neither was intelligence. Relevant knowledge—in this case, exposure to innovators and the specific practices of innovation—had a big impact.[10]

One Step Forward, One Step Back

Meanwhile, there is another, more straightforward reason why three- and four-year-olds might falter in the classic hook challenge. Maybe inventing for its own sake is just not that appealing to them. To test this possibility, my student Whitney Sandford and I presented four- and five-year-olds with an appealing array of materials: wooden blocks of different shapes and sizes, marbles, ramps, Play-Doh, Silly Putty, tape, wooden wheels, dowels, colored pipe cleaners, and K'nex pieces. In one condition of the experiment, we invited children simply to play with the materials. In another condition, having made sure they knew the meaning of the word "invent," we invited them to use the materials to invent something. Somewhat surprisingly, the children who were not prompted to invent but simply invited to play engaged in more invention, and were far more focused on the goals of their inventions.[11]

Not only that, children in the play condition talked a lot more about what they wanted to make, and how they were making it. Children in the invent condition had trouble describing or explaining their creations. When Whitney asked them what they were making, they'd often respond "I don't know." In contrast, children in the play condition spontaneously announced their goals out loud, identifying the problems they wanted to solve before they even began to handle the materials. One little girl eagerly announced, "I'm going to make a butterfly on a rainbow!" A little boy explained that he would use the toys to build bridges because his old house was on a river. Another girl set to work building her family's house. Notably, she verbally planned each step and tried out different materials to find the most suitable ones for each task. For instance, she asked herself, "What can be a blankie?" and explored multiple options before ultimately deciding to fashion a blanket out of Silly Putty for her parents' bedroom.

In a subsequent experiment, we invited eighty children between the ages of four and six to use materials to help a toy figure cross a bridge to save another character. The setup was playful and dramatic, offering a wide range of materials and latitude for each child to come up with solutions in his or her own way. All eighty children used the materials to devise a way to get over the river, a remarkable success rate. Many came up with ingenious solutions, marking a surprising contrast to the studies involving the hook task. It may be, then, that while children can invent when they are quite young, they struggle with doing so on demand. Consciously harnessing one's skills at rethinking reality to solve someone else's problem may take more time and emotional maturity than the youngest inventors possess.[12]

However, just as one part of the process of invention becomes easier, another psychological challenge emerges. Consider the following example. A six-year-old named Eva has built a lemonade stand from two cardboard boxes in front of her building. She wants a bell so that customers can call her when she isn't behind the stand. It must be loud enough for her to hear even if she wanders to her neighbor's stoop, so that she can come running back to make the sale. But she has no bell. She knows there could be a substitute—something else that makes a ringing sound if you hit it. She understands the structure of the problem. But looking around, she doesn't see anything remotely bell-like. She sees paper cups that have toppled out of the garbage, a broken bike lock lying on the pavement, and a bucket with gardening tools near the flower box her mother has just been tending—but nothing she can use. By now, her four-year-old cousin, Margy, has paused from riding her scooter and taken an interest in the problem. She quickly spies the gardening bucket, lifts two small trowels out of it and trumpets, "Eva, look. Look—I've got bells!" Eva stares. "Those aren't bells," she informs her cousin. "They're my mom's shovels." Just as children become better at identifying the problem they want to solve, they also become less open-minded.

It turns out there is a reason for this intellectual loss, albeit an unexpected one. Imagine hoisting up your two-year-old grandchild, niece, or daughter to sit on the counter while you beat a few eggs. She watches with interest as you crack the shells and dump the yolks and whites into the bowl. She pays close attention to the whisk, which she has never seen before, as you pull it from the drawer, dip it into the bowl and begin whisking. You might think that the objects themselves—the wiggly yolks, the fragile shells, the wiry whisk—would absorb all of her attention. Not so. She is equally attuned to what you are trying to do. Experiments have shown that babies are surprisingly able to detect human intention, which they use to guide their own interactions with objects.[13] In one study, for instance, eighteen-month-old babies watched a small human-like robot try and attach two parts of an attractive bright toy, but just before the two parts connected (via a magnet), the robot missed. Then the experimenter offered the two toy parts to the young subjects, who quickly finished the task for the robot. One might argue that rather than helping the robot achieve "his goal," the toddlers were merely following through on the obvious next step. In a second condition, however, toddlers were shown the same connection failure, but by a machine that bore no resemblance to a human. Presented with this version, toddlers were interested and watched carefully, but did not complete the sequence afterwards. From this we can surmise that, when the toddlers did connect the two parts of the toy, it was to help another who appeared to have a goal. Children's quick grasp of human intention determined what they did with the two toy parts.[14]

That ability to detect human intention is a pivotal moment in development because it allows children to get some purchase on the world of people and people-made objects. And here the developmental plot thickens. Although babies can infer a person's intention with regard to *using* an object, it will be several more years before they figure out that some objects were *designed* for a particular use. A toddler doesn't distinguish between natural objects and artifacts—objects made with a purpose in mind. For instance, a sixteen-month-old is quick to notice her father piling plates on top of each other while clearing the dinner table, or using a rake to pull leaves into a pile. But she would not draw a clear distinction between a rock and a pestle as tools to grind nuts; both can do the job, and that's all she notices. She's aware of the actions a particular object affords. She's also aware of what a person might intend to do with an object. But she's happily oblivious to the notion of an object's having been designed by someone for a purpose.

And that obliviousness is something of an asset when it comes to invention. Thanks to some intricate experimental sleuthing, we know more about why. In one revealing study, Tim German and Greta Defeyter invited children ages five through seven to sit at a table on which there were various small objects: a puppet, a plastic dog wedged into a long, clear, plastic tube, and some other toys. They told each young subject a story about Sam the puppet, who wanted to take a long journey on his spaceship. The child was then shown some of the things that Sam was taking along on his journey, including the straw, the pencil, a pad of paper, a cup, a ping-pong ball, and a plastic ruler. In one condition, the children were shown the purpose of the cup and the straw. The experimenter demonstrated how Sam could drink out of the cup using the straw, and write on the pad using the pencil. In a second condition, children were not taught the purpose of the straw and the pencil. Next, in both conditions, the experimenter explained to each child that Sam's naughty dog, named Tog, had run away and gotten stuck in a clear tube. Then the experimenter asked each child, "Can you help Sam by getting Tog out of the tube?"[15]

Here is where the experiment's intricacy paid off. In the first condition, the children had learned the intended design of both the pencil and the straw; only one (the pencil) was long and thin enough to help get Tog out of the tube. Younger participants chose the pencil to free Tog, whether they had learned its purpose or not. They were focused on which object had the features that would render it useful for the task. But older children were hampered by the information that the pencil was for writing. Their newly acquired sense of design was something of a handicap.

Eva, at six, had lost her ability to see that a shovel might also be a bell, but her cousin Margy, who didn't yet think in terms of intended function, was freer to solve the lemonade stand problem. The research points to a seemingly abstruse but actually central idea: until children are about six, they are relatively unconstrained by any awareness that a human-built object was designed by someone for an intended purpose. And that delay in acquiring a "theory of design" makes the younger children more open to alternative uses of objects.

Such openness clearly has great value. In many tests of creativity, the more that people can free themselves of the intended purpose of an object (a pen, a fork, a stick, etc.), the more varied their ideas will be, and the higher their creativity scores.[16] Children's naivete about the world offers them another even more obscure but essential strength when it comes to innovation—they are somewhat more freewheeling in deciding what might work.[17] Their flexibility is useful in another way as well—it makes them quite nimble when it comes to a critical tool in the process of invention: causal reasoning.

Whodunnit? Learning to Identify Causes

At a remarkably young age, babies construct hypotheses about the world and use those hypotheses to guide their actions. As part of this, they are disposed to generalize beyond the immediate objects and actions in front of them and develop overarching concepts and abstract theories about how things work. For instance, children figure out that open or hollow objects float in water while closed, heavy objects sink; that small things balance best on top of large things; that, if an object has a hole in it, they can stick something in there. In one set of studies, for example, children aged thirty months to four years watched an experimenter lift blocks of different shapes and colors and touch them to a "Blicket detector." It was a machine that played music and flashed lights when touched by certain blocks. After watching the experimenter test a few blocks, only some of which activated it, children as young as four could readily predict which other blocks would make the machine work, and must therefore be "blickets." Children quickly decipher patterns and rules that help them to be efficient and successful. Inferring "blicketness" is an example of one of the first kinds of theory-building they engage in.[18]

It's powerful, but it's not enough. Many daily experiences are so complex they require a strategy just to figure out what kind of causal theory will help make sense of the events in question. Consider the following example. A little girl and her older brother, ages five and seven, were awake in their bedroom long after their mother had fallen asleep in her room. They heard a door open, and some footsteps. Then they heard more footsteps and a door open and close. They became certain a stranger was in the house. They lay in their beds whispering to each other, trying to figure out just how scared they should be. Their account the next morning made it clear they tried out different theories on one another. Possibly a murderer had come in, killed their mother, and then escaped. Or perhaps the murderer did not leave . . . it could be it wasn't just one . . . and maybe they were now heading for the children's bedroom. As if they had not worked themselves into enough of a frenzy of fear, next they heard chopping. What could explain this new twist? Finally, they crawled out of bed and, holding hands, crept from their room toward the kitchen. There they found their two teenage cousins, who had separately come home within a few moments of one another and decided to cook a late dinner.

Similar mysteries arise on a daily basis (though most of them don't elicit such lurid or charged speculations). The underlying thinking required in these situations is common, and very important. Presented with something unexpected, we want and need to figure out what caused it. Sometimes the best strategy is to single out the most likely cause from many possible causes. Imagine, for instance, that it's a hot, muggy night in your suburb and you hear a rumble of thunder. The electric power goes out, and you want to know why. It might be that a lightning strike has brought a tree down on a wire. It might be that a whole town turning up its air conditioning has caused a brownout. It could be a problem with just your own fuse box. You seriously doubt it was caused by more than one of these happening at once. Psychologists call this a *disjunctive* causal hypothesis. Making the assumption that there is one cause to be identified helps us simplify the world and act effectively. But some situations call for a different kind of causal theory. The authors of one study offer the example of a microwave. Making it work requires both plugging it in and turning it on. There are two causes, both necessary, neither sufficient.[19] If you suspect you are dealing with this kind of situation, psychologists say you have a *conjunctive* causal hypothesis. In some cases, it is the better kind of theory to have. And here, young children have the advantage.

Adults tend to think most things have one cause or another, and that in any situation they must figure out which one is responsible. This strategy often works, but not always. Recall the young children who were so adept at figuring out which blocks would activate a machine. In another study using the same kind of "detector" as that one, researchers made the task more complicated, and compared adults to children. Once again, subjects were shown a machine and told that some of the blocks, placed on top of it, would activate it. But this time, it wasn't possible to activate it with any one block; making it respond required certain combinations of two blocks. For the most part, the adults were stumped, because they stuck with a disjunctive causal hypothesis. The children, however, approached the problem more flexibly. When first presented with the puzzle, they too tended to try one kind of block at a time. But when that didn't work, they shifted to the other kind of strategy, using a "conjunctive" theory, trying different combinations of types of blocks. The younger children's advantage was that they were able to go back and forth between the two kinds of hypotheses, depending on the situation.[20]

Why would children be better than adults at sussing out the correct explanation? Christopher Lucas and his colleagues suggest that the disjunctive rule is more common. Because adults simply have more life experience than children, they are more stuck on the explanation they have experienced time and again.[21] In other words, when it comes to causal explanations, children's relative innocence renders them more responsive to the actual scene in front of them, and less constrained by what they "know" from prior experience. It's just one good example of the way in which children, however limited in some aspects of idea building, have certain advantages, by virtue of their naivete. Their inexperience also helps explain another essential item in the toolkit of invention.

The Value of Copycatting

Back to Cora, whom we last saw trying again and again with no success to catch a lizard with a stick. Now, Cora's older brother, Frankie, age six, wanders over and watches. "You're just *poking* them with that stick," he mutters. "You need to *grab* 'em." Frankie took two sticks and tried to use them together like chopsticks or tweezers. Cora watched him for a minute, and then tried it herself. She may not have been able to identify the "parameters of the problem," but she knew how to imitate her brother.

Recall that Beck and Apperly's research showed that, although children had trouble figuring out how to reach the prize on their own, they were quite adept at it once they saw a grownup do it first. They are deft imitators.[22] And overall, that's a good thing. In fact, psychologists believe that the human inclination to imitate what other humans do accounts for our ability to build and transmit culture. Not only do we imitate, which other species do, we over-imitate, which is unique to our species. In one study, researchers showed young children and wild-born chimpanzees how to get a prize from an opaque box.[23] The experimenter poked a stick through a hole on the top, then opened a small door on the side of the box and used the stick to pull out the prize. Both the chimps and the three- and four-year-olds faithfully copied both actions when it was their turn, lowering the stick through the narrow hole and opening the door on the side. Then, another set of chimps and children were shown the same sequence, except that, for them, the box was not opaque but transparent. In this condition it was clear to see that poking the stick through the top didn't have anything to do with getting the prize. Here, a difference emerged. The chimps ignored the first, ineffective action and imitated only the effective one (opening the door and using the stick to fish out the prize). The children, however, faithfully copied both actions they had observed—the one that mattered and the one that didn't.

Our desire to join the world of others can limit our capacity to invent, especially when we are very young. As children get older, they get savvier at figuring out when it's better not to imitate and instead to come up with their own solutions. Kayleigh Carr and her colleagues have shown that four-year-olds imitate an adult's approach to devising tools even when the adult makes mistakes. But by the time children are eight, they only imitate when the adult's innovation meets with success, choosing to devise their own tools when the adult fails.[24]

Copying Frankie had brought Cora closer to catching a lizard. But it still was not enough. Frankie ran into the kitchen and brought back a variety of cooking utensils—some metal tongs, a spatula, and a small sieve. The two children tried the tongs, but they were too slow and clumsy to work with. Cora tried slapping the spatula down as a lizard rushed past. Frankie was dismissive of that approach: "That'll just smash him." Frankie lifted up the sieve like a net, waiting for the lizard to reappear. When it did, he brought the sieve down. But the lizard was still too quick, darting easily out of reach.

Luckily, both Frankie and Cora had a skill that comes in handy in this situation: they were experienced at combining familiar elements in new ways. Even toddlers can cobble together actions they have taken before into new sequences. If they've learned how to stack several blocks, and they've played at rolling a ball back and forth, they can easily progress on their own to a new game of bowling a ball into a block tower. This early capacity for recombination, which begins in play, underlies the more sophisticated process of generating novel sentences out of familiar words and phrases. Jerome Bruner argued that those early combinations of physical moves provided children with a "grammar of action"—sequences of gestures that contained subject, object, and verb, and gave children an entrée into the world of syntax.[25]

Francys Subiaul and his colleagues have found that children can apply this recombination technique to new experiences as well as to words and gestures they already know. In one of their studies, two adults showed each child a complicated wooden box containing a nice sticker. The drawer with the sticker could be accessed only by manipulating more than one part of the box. Each child watched as one adult demonstrated one of the necessary actions, then the other adult demonstrated the second necessary action. Even the three- and four-year-olds quickly figured out that they'd have to copy both adults to get the sticker—a skill psychologists call "summative imitation." By that they mean that children not only can imitate various small actions and gestures, but that they can combine these actions to achieve a new goal. And in that way, even the preschooler invents like a pro.[26]

Cora looked at the short-handled sieve for a moment and said, "Let's tape it on the stick!" Running back into the kitchen, she found a roll of tape, and the two children worked together to bind the two parts together. Now they had a tool that was long enough and could scoop. At four, Cora was mentally flexible enough to see that something with two different features, both essential, was needed. She and Frankie waited stealthily with their new trap. When the next lizard appeared from under the rock and began to scurry across the stones, Frankie extended the new device far out in front of it and dropped the sieve. The trapped lizard rushed right up into the metal net, and Frankie scooped it triumphantly. They had tamed the dragon. Could Cora have done it alone? Perhaps not, but probably neither could Frankie.

On the Shoulders of Very Young Giants

Mark Nielsen has pointed out that one of the more impressive aspects of human invention is that we almost never invent in a vacuum, instead almost always building on the inventions of others. This happens only because we are able to learn from those around us, copy their creations, and detect their intended uses of objects. In his words, "A key feature of human culture is not only that skills are readily transmitted from one generation to the next but that such skills are modified and improved on, sometimes at a remarkable pace." He goes on to offer a wonderful example of that speed: "Consider Clément Ader, who in 1890 made the first manned, powered, heavier-than-air flight. This was certainly a remarkable achievement, but it took less than 80 years to go from his bat-wing monoplane to a craft capable of putting Neil Armstrong and Edwin Aldrin on the moon."[27]

Young children seem to practice an early form of building on the inventions of others. Watch any group of four-year-olds engage in pretend play and you will notice that, once one of them designates a hairbrush to serve as a telephone, the others readily and steadily use it as a telephone during that episode of play. They note one another's transformations of objects—accepting what others imagine an object can be and not just what it is—and they build on that.

We often think of inventors as oddballs and nerds, tinkering away in their solitary labs (or muddy roads, as the case may be). But most of the time, scientists do not work alone. They collaborate, exchange data, attempt to replicate and refine one another's findings, and build on previous work. Children are just the same.

Two Inventors Are Better Than One

If you think about Cora's lizard quest, you'll note that the moment her brother became interested in it, Cora's options multiplied. That happens all the time. Back in the 1970s, people who happened to walk past the room where Daniel Kahneman was working with his long-time collaborator, Amos Tversky, were likely to hear ebullient chatter and great deal of laughter. Kahneman and Tversky, famous for their pioneering work on how people arrive at judgments about what to do or not to do in everyday life, often sat together batting around ideas. They loved working together. But it was more than fun. They realized that talking together strengthened each one's ideas immeasurably. As Cass Sunstein and Richard Thaler put it, "they did not really know where one's thought ended and the other's began."[28] And like children at play, the process of finding the solution was as satisfying to them as the solution itself. Kahneman said about his own research, "I get a sense of movement and discovery whenever I find a flaw in my thinking."[29] When it comes to scientific inventions, two or three minds are often better than one. And children are uniquely suited to make use of the power of collaborative problem-solving.

Invention

Henry had a problem. His fly wouldn't stay shut. Day in and day out, he'd pull on his jeans, button up his shirt, slip into his sneakers, and march off to fourth grade, only to look down and find his zipper had crept southward. He'd yank it up. If he was with other boys, he didn't think much of it. Sometimes they all had a good laugh at their wayward zippers. If there were girls around, it wasn't quite so funny. What if they teased him? What if they saw his underwear peeking through? He'd surreptitiously sidle over to a corner of the classroom, behind a plant or some bookshelves, and pull it back up, pressing down the little metal tag that was supposed to insure it would remain in place. His mother sometimes saw his hand drift toward his zipper and quickly, delicately pat it to make sure it was closed.

It was just a small problem, like many that plague children at school: lost homework, farts, disloyal friends, soggy sandwiches. But, when his fourth-grade teacher announced that everyone in the class should think of something that needed a better solution, because they were going to spend the next month inventing things, it was the problem that came to Henry's mind. His buddy, Harry, signed on to the project instantly. Henry had come to the school at midyear, not knowing anyone. Harry was bolder than Henry, a bit of a show-off, but he longed for a best buddy. On Henry's very first day, Harry sensed the kind of chemistry that makes for dynamic duos in fourth grade. New to the school, Henry was thrilled to have a fast friend. It pretty much went without saying that they would be working together.

Henry had been the one to name the problem they should work on, but it was Harry who collected the possibly useful materials— including electrical tape, wooden tongue depressors, fabric, and string. They talked and talked, looked at their zippers, talked some more, and began assembling a prototype for their invention—which Henry had now branded the Zipper Tipper. They wrapped several feet of tape around one of the tongue depressors until they had something that seemed heavy enough to provide a counterweight to the gravitational pull of the zipper tab. They attached this weight to a sturdy cord, also fabricated out of tape. To the cord, they added a string slender enough to thread through a hole in the snap fixture of a pair of jeans and knot onto the zipper tab. Their Zipper Tipper was ready.

As their friends gathered round, only too happy to critique the design—it wouldn't work, it was too heavy, it was cumbersome, it would create its own problems—Harry objected. The Zipper Tipper might not have been his idea, but he was its staunch defender. It was just right as is. It would keep a zipper closed. It was not too big, too long, or too heavy. Everyone argued about it until, finally, the boys' teacher stepped in. "You need to try it out," Ms. Fanelli said, zeroing in on Harry as the more obstinate and vocal of the team. "You won't know if it really works or not until you wear it."

Harry was game. The next day, he brought in a pair of jeans and they attached the Zipper Tipper. The day after that, he came in wearing the contraption. Sure enough, it banged against him, pulled the waist of his pants, and created a whole new set of problems. Harry and Henry would have to return to the drawing board. At their teacher's suggestion, they discussed its design problems. At some point in their conversation over the next several days (constantly interrupted as they were by math, reading, gym, and the rest), Harry and Henry began to agree that modifying their design wouldn't help. If they made the Zipper Tipper small and light enough to avoid the other problems, it wouldn't hold the zipper up. And they couldn't think of a way of keeping it from swinging around as the wearer walked.

Ms. Fanelli suggested they give up on their first design and zero in on some other approach, urging them to think about the various reasons a zipper might drop down. After several fleeting discussions that fizzled out, Henry had an idea. "We don't need to weigh it down," he mused. "We just need to stop it from moving." Harry jumped on that thought: "We could create a barrier." A little girl lingering nearby who overheard the two boys' conversation chimed in, "You guys need Velcro." By the next day, they had designed a Zipper Tipper that worked—even if it was no longer a tipper but a stopper. Small flaps of fabric sewn to both sides of the zipper's top could be closed over the zipper once it was all the way up, preventing it from sliding down.

The Zipper Tipper represents a whole new stage of invention, quite different from the fleeting and fairly limited inventions of three- and four-year-olds. Henry and Harry spent days, not just moments, on their project. It involved deliberation, revision, and reflection. It also involved other people. Probably Henry and Harry would never have tried to solve Henry's zipper problem if someone hadn't asked them to invent something, and to begin by thinking of a problem to solve. Their teacher also carved out significant time for them to work on it, and suggested a crucial step—testing out the first prototype. But it wasn't only Ms. Fanelli who weighed in. Other children were interested in their friends' efforts and felt free to watch and kibitz. While too much help can stifle invention by encouraging imitation—especially for younger children—the right level and kinds of input (suggestions, challenges, and encouragement) improve both the process and the outcome.

Taken together, the studies described in these pages provide a view into the minds of the youngest inventors. A full assortment of intellectual tools is required for invention, including skills in imitation, the ability to identify the structure of a problem, the psychological and actual transformation of objects, and the flexibility to either accept or overlook the intended use of an object. These strengths develop together in a see-saw manner, and eventually combine into complex capabilities.

The research also reveals that, although children begin inventing when they are very young, their powers of innovation are limited in some nonobvious ways. Their proclivity to imitate, for example, is both the friend and foe of invention. Their attunement to the design and intended purpose of objects is a mixed blessing, too. They are not very good at structuring a problem in a way that makes it solvable. This in part explains why they are likely to tackle only the most practical and immediate problems, such as cookie jars well out of reach or bath toys that won't sink.

At the same time, young children are less constrained than older children and adults by repertoires of explanations and theories about the nature of explanations. This makes them more likely to pay attention to the data in front of them. Not only does this allow them to identify somewhat unexpected explanatory principles (such as conjunctive rather than disjunctive causes), it also allows them to come up with fairly novel uses of objects. The limitations that three- and four-year-olds face when dealing with ill-structured problems are balanced by their open-mindedness. It takes a while for all these inclinations and skills to come together; children can only orchestrate the full set of skills needed to be true inventors when they are about eight or nine years old. But to accurately see the role of invention in mental development, a wide lens is necessary. An inventory of school-aged inventions would reveal a broad range of gadgets, habitats, and games—but also music, sagas, societies, and even athletic events.

It didn't always rain in Conewego. There were plenty of long summer days when young Roger Bolton was left to occupy himself, or had to drive the tractor for his dad (which he did from a very early age). On those days, building water systems wasn't an option. Growing up on that isolated farm, Roger vividly recalls the mythical baseball and football teams he created and the long, detailed games he narrated in his mind as he sat on the tractor or waited for his dad to get home. His favorite imaginary team was called the Red Sox, though he had never been to Boston. He still remembers the players he came up with: James "Stretch" Stanley was the first baseman, Fred Simms played third base, the shortstop was Grover Lands. "I laid out whole games from beginning to end, thinking through each play: *Stretch makes a diving catch and ends the inning!*" Roger was not athletic himself, but loved sports and read many biographies of players. He followed several teams with the help of the local newspaper his father read every day. "I knew the rules, and I had a lot of information about each sport," he recalls, "even if I couldn't play them."

Inventions come in many shapes and sizes. Mental inventions like stories, imaginary sports, and music draw on many of the same intellectual elements as creating gadgets and tools. In each case, a child must identify a problem that they want to solve. They must recognize that the solution requires something new or unavailable—a gadget, a tool, a notational system, a story, or a scenario. They must be able to work through a problem, whether that work takes sixty seconds or six days, trying out various combinations of elements, testing possible solutions against the problem, revising when needed, and recognizing when their invention has succeeded.

By age nine, children have nearly all the necessary intellectual skills to be creative and clever in their inventions. Whether they use these skills to come up with novel objects and contraptions depends in part on the opportunities they have had along the way. The road to intermittent windshield wipers, better economic policies, and gene separators begins when we are three. Alma Deuthscher, born in 2005, has for years already been an acclaimed pianist, violinist, and composer. She composed her first piano sonata when she was six. Even a prodigy like Alma draws on what she comes up with while at play. One profile about her reports that, at age four, "she would sit for hours at the piano, working out melodies she said were songs from the imaginary world she called Transylvanian."[30]

Makeshift step stools, pails that act as submarines, devices that retrieve prizes from hard-to-reach places, imaginary lands, and zipper tippers help children become good thinkers. But the products of invention are not limited to such tangible solutions. As an old man, looking back on a life of scholarship, Roger Bolton tilts his head, struck by a realization: "You know, my scientific interest in economic systems began in the mud outside my parents' home."

4

Ideas

Do you know why I can't sleep at night, Mummie? Shall I tell
you? It's because I think of things.

—Four-year-old Ursula, as quoted by Susan Isaacs

Addie collected bugs and bones. Roger played in the mud. But at
some point, tactile explorations and hands-on inventions lead to a different kind of intellectual work: children begin to inhabit the world
of abstract ideas. That developmental transition has, for the most part,
flown under the adult radar. Perhaps that's because the ideas that shape
our lives also fly under the radar. And often, the more potent the idea,
the more invisible it is.

Some time in my late twenties I began to dream about a house.
I had the dream not once, not twice, but again and again—perhaps,
over the years, fifty or sixty times. In the dream, I'd be inside my house.
It was always disappointingly suburban and pedestrian. Sometimes it
was a split-level house, like the one in Steven Spielberg's *Poltergeist*. It
seemed ugly to me, ghastly even, with its windowless, cheaply deco-
rated rooms. In my dream, I felt disappointed that this was my home.
How had I ended up in a structure like this—not to my taste, but
boring, stale, and cheesy? Sometimes I'd panic: How could I be living
in such a wrong house? Then I'd wake up and be in my real house—an

old barn that my husband and I had renovated with our own four hands—a house that felt totally me, which I loved beyond anything, as rural and quirky as you could get. The euphoria I felt in that moment was worth the momentary panic during the dream.

After I had had this dream several times, when I was, say, thirty-two or so, I told my mother about it. She got a funny smile on her face. A smile that said *I know something about you now, but I won't say what.*

"What?" I demanded. "What does that smile mean?"

"That dream is about your marriage."

Huh, I thought. *Really?* It didn't feel like that to me. But she was in her sixties, I was in my thirties, and she was the one who had been in psychoanalysis, not me. I wasn't totally sure she was wrong. So I said nothing. And I kept on dreaming of houses.

By the time I was in my forties, the dream had expanded. I'd be in the possibly split-level and definitely cheesy house, unhappy and queasy with disappointment. Then I'd notice a door or hallway I hadn't seen before. Sometimes another person, a friend or relative, would suggest we walk through there, into a part of the house I hadn't known existed. Often there were many rooms in this part of the house. Sometimes they were lovely and spacious, and other times dusty or dank, with moldy, ancient wallpaper. Seeing them, I'd be suffused with a strange mixture of unease and elation.

It felt creepy. What might I find in the rooms I had yet to explore? What if they contained awful things—dead animals, rotten food, broken furniture? Often the me in the dream would feel disturbed that I had been living all this time in a house that contained rooms of which I had been unaware. As if someone unseen had been watching me. But at the same time, I'd also feel exhilarated by how big my house was. I'd sit on a couch in one of the newly revealed rooms and think over my options: one could be my study, one a dining room. I could use lots of them for guest rooms, I could even have a second kitchen. The options seemed endless, and so alluring. As I got older, the thrill of those mysterious rooms began to outweigh my dissatisfaction with the house's ugliness. The creepiness receded, and with each recurrence I became exultant at the feeling of endless possibility those rooms offered me.

My son, Will, had his own recurrent dream. He dreamt again and again of wild animals. As a boy, in his dreams he'd fight them or they'd attack him. During his teens, he began dreaming that he was embracing the animals. Other times, they'd tear him to shreds. Once, in early adulthood, he dreamt of a large beast, part wolf and part moose, that shrank until it was a teensy-weensy creature, no longer a threat.

I finally said to him, "You're dreaming of your impulses."

"Ya think?" He looked at me with cool skepticism. "What about *your* dream, huh? What's that?"

I suddenly knew with total clarity what my dream had meant all along. The house *was* my unconscious. The rooms embodied the parts of my mind that were, for the most part, hidden from me. Naturally, I thought to myself, my unconscious thoughts and feelings, like those unexpected rooms, were a little scary. No surprise that those darker, more turbulent thoughts, lurking just beneath the surface, made me uneasy. Knowing I had such feelings, but not really confronting them, was just like finding out you lived in a house with a room you had not known existed. And just like in the dream, the chance to delve into my wilder more daring thoughts was not merely unsettling, it was also exciting. It offered me an adventure, very akin to entering some mysterious and attractive room one had never seen before. I grabbed my son's arm.

"Oh my god! I know what my dream means. The rooms? They're my unconscious." I gleefully announced. I told him, too, about his grandmother telling me all those years before that the dream was my ambivalence at getting married so young.

"That wasn't it at all," I said. "I knew that wasn't right. It never felt like her interpretation fit."

His eyes crinkled. "You're kidding right? Her interpretation and yours, they're the same."

"No, she thought the dream was about my youthful marriage," I protested. "But that's not it. The rooms represent my own inner mind. That's so, *so* different!"

"Nope," he smiled knowingly. "Either way—your dream and mine, your mother's interpretation or yours—all versions of the same idea."

He was right—the three generations were all talking about the way in which our dreams reveal the feelings and thoughts we are unable and unwilling to acknowledge in waking life. The idea of the unconscious is so big and so pervasive, it has become invisible. But that hasn't always been the case.

Freud's formulation of the unconscious first crystallized in 1896, as he sat in his study trying to make sense of his patients' complaints. The basic outlines of that story are familiar to many. Trained as a physician, he became interested in the mysterious symptoms some of his patients exhibited—incessant coughing, loss of appetite, lethargy, limbs that didn't work correctly. He could see for himself that their suffering was real. Yet no physical cause could explain their problems. Deeply influenced first by the work of the neurologist Jean-Marie Charcot and later by the physician Josef Breuer, he began to form a first draft of his theory. He reasoned that his patients had suffered various kinds of sexual trauma at the hands of relatives or other adults—trauma that had left no physical mark, and had, in fact, been forgotten. Those buried memories of abuse, he believed, had eventually caused physical symptoms. But many of his colleagues and friends—including Breuer, whom he so admired—rejected his theory. They claimed it to be unwieldy, preposterous, and convoluted.

Freud alternated between vehement conviction and a nagging sense of uncertainty. At some point he began to doubt himself. Could it really be, he wondered, that so many of his patients had endured sexual assault as very young children? It seemed so unlikely. His self-doubt could have led him in a different direction. He might, for instance, have concluded the patients were simply pretending, or malingering, as it was often called in the late nineteenth century. Or he might have conjectured that specific physical causes which he simply hadn't yet uncovered explained each patient's symptom. But that's not where his thoughts took him. Instead, he began to consider the opposite possibility: maybe he hadn't taken his nascent idea far enough. Perhaps it wasn't that his patients had suffered assaults as children and forgotten them. Maybe their symptoms were not the result of buried memories, but instead the result of buried feelings and thoughts. Freud biographer Peter Gay describes this as the period in Freud's life when psychoanalysis was born.[1] That may be true. But, at the very same time, something else even more revolutionary was taking shape in Freud's thoughts: the idea of the unconscious mind itself.

The notion of unseen psychological forces driving human behavior wasn't totally new when Freud hit upon it. First glimmers can be found in Galen's work during the second century in Greece. Galen argued that there were four temperaments affecting all individuals. Each of the temperaments was caused by an imbalance in one of four bodily fluids, which had been described by Hippocrates: blood, black bile, yellow bile, and phlegm.[2] A century later, in nearby Iran, one of the founders of modern medicine, Avicenna, also argued for the role that bodily fluids played in shaping a person's moods and personality.[3] But then the notion went underground. For the next eight centuries, all over the globe, people's feelings and actions were believed either to be caused by spirit forces or to be completely within one's deliberate conscious control—either God's fault or your own. The idea of the unconscious went dormant for a long time.

Then, in the mid-nineteenth century, the idea peeked out once again. In 1866, German physicist Hermann von Helmholtz offered his scientific colleagues an explanation for why people persist in certain beliefs even when they know better. He used the example of our perception that the sun sinks below the horizon each night, even though we know that, in fact, it is the earth that is turning. He argued that our experience is shaped by assumptions that remain out of reach of our rational deliberate knowledge and thoughts. Such thoughts bedevil one's everyday thinking, von Helmholtz claimed, no matter how educated one is, or how deliberately and methodically one tries to render judgments. He referred to these powerful yet invisible biases as *unbewusster Schluss*—unconscious conclusions or inferences.[4] His work was ignored by other scientists, who considered it unimportant at best, preposterous at worst. Less than thirty years later, the idea would reappear yet again, in a new form, part of an intellectual tsunami which was gathering force in the heart of sedate Vienna.

When Freud announced that his patients' symptoms were failed efforts to repress unwanted thoughts, he opened up a whole new way of thinking about the human psyche. He argued that there is an architecture to the human mind—and that this structure includes a cellar teeming with thoughts and feelings. Those thoughts and feelings, barely contained, threaten everyday functioning. Forbidden by society to give voice to them, most of us do everything we can to keep them under wraps, hidden not only from others but even from ourselves. Freud cast our own internal suppression of them as the watchman guarding the entrance to the main part of the house. Each of us, he argued, labors incessantly in an effort to keep the forbidden thoughts locked behind the cellar door. That effort is taxing enough to make some people physically sick—hence, the coughs, the partial paralysis, the fatigue.

But ever since Freud bestowed this new way of thinking upon us, we've been trying to get rid of the gift. To many it has seemed an out-landish idea, riddled with unprovable claims. It was yoked to other, even more absurd theories—the Oedipus and Electra complexes, penis envy and castration anxiety, and the constant probing of dreams as a way of purging troubling and troublesome repressed thoughts. To be sure, Freud's thinking has had its waves of devoted practitioners and believers. In general, however, people have dismissed most of it as far-fetched, narrowminded, sexist, and unsupported by data. It would be another hundred years before the modern field of empirical psy-chology would unintentionally return to Freud's idea.

How Ideas Begin

Ideas with the force and magnitude of the unconscious may be few and far between, but they are merely the pinnacle of a common and ubiquitous process. The ability to form an idea is not the province of intellectual giants alone. Ordinary men and women have ideas day in and day out. Imagine pausing on a city street corner and watching people go by, some of them laughing with friends, others staring at smartphones as they walk, a few looking at the buildings they pass, some hurrying to appointments. Some of them appear to be doing nothing much at all, just lost in thought. At least a few of those pass-ersby are mulling over an idea as you watch them. It may be an idea they encountered in a book or a podcast (say, the cause of political polarization in the United States, or the roots of alcoholism). It may be an idea their partner floated by them at breakfast (why friendships change over time), or they may be coming up with one of their own (the situations in which machines cannot replace humans, or the causes of voter apathy). A few among us may be crafting an idea that will turn out to be lasting and noteworthy. But most ideas are fleeting and insignificant. The difference between those with influential ideas and the rest of us, whose ideas are small and transitory, is not particularly instructive, resting on factors that are out of our control (luck, timing, extraordinary intelligence). But there is a far more interesting difference that cries out for explanation. Why is it that by adulthood, only some people are drawn to pursuing ideas, while most are not? The answer to this question lies in childhood—when we first begin to have ideas.[5]

I have already argued that, even when very young children are digging around in a pile of mud or cobbling together a new fort, they are learning to deal with complexity and solve problems. But these activities also pave the way for more obviously intellectual work, though it may not appear so to the adult eye. Even in childhood, it's not all poking, tying, and stacking. By the time they are three years old, children are also examining propositions, pondering elusive phenomena, and connecting familiar information in new ways. The rest of this chapter explores the kinds of ideas young children think about. Such intellectual projects begin with the deceptively simple process of mulling things over.

Several years ago, an old friend took her six-year-old goddaughter, Ella, out for a treat. They drove along chatting about this and that for quite a while. They talked about first grade, soccer, and Ella's little sister. But then Ella lapsed into silence. She had a distracted and slightly dreamy look on her face. She barely seemed to notice when the car finally stopped and her godmother came around to the passenger side to help her out of the car. Ella was staring out the window, but not looking at anything in particular. Her godmother, struck by her silent look of absorption, asked, "What are you doing?"

"I'm thinking," Ella answered in a faraway voice.

Her godmother pressed for more. "What're you thinking about?"

"Candy," she said, turning back to her thoughts. "I need a little more time."

Daydreaming about candy may not seem, at first blush, like the first step toward having an idea. And yet it contains elements that are key to the process of forming one. Ella was lost in thought, unaware of the events around her, focused instead on the images unfolding in her mind. During her sugary reveries, she wasn't acting on her thoughts (asking or looking for candy in the car), she was content simply to be thinking them. She may have been sorting images into categories— chocolate and fruity, chewy and crunchy, or maybe good and bad—a kind of intellectual work necessary to any idea that uses facts. Perhaps she was imagining scenarios, another essential tool for complex thinking, in which she may have been eating, concocting, or constructing things out of candy. Children's first ideas are not formally organized like those of philosophers or scientists. And three- and four-year-olds may not always be aware that they *are* pursuing ideas. Ella realized she needed more time for her thoughts, but for others such deliberate consideration and metacognition come later. The earliest contemplations may set the stage for the more organized purposeful projects of mature intellectual life. Without a finished product (an invention or a proposition) it can be hard to know when children are engaged in intellectual pursuits. Often the only sign we have of it comes from the questions they ask.

Young children don't ask questions only about bugs, bones, and shiny things. They also, from the first, ask questions probing topics that are neither immediate nor concrete. Shortly before I began work on this book, I was on an airplane and sitting behind a young mother and her very small daughter, who was about three or four years old. We were already high up in the sky. The little girl was staring out the window, her face smashed up against it so she could see the ground far below. "Mommy," she mused, "there's probably a little kid down there asking *her* mommy if there is a kid up here in a plane. And is her mommy going to say yes, there *is* a child up there?"

Far earlier than psychologists might be aware, young children begin constructing mental objects of contemplation.[6] The little girl on the plane had some inkling that two people could have very similar thoughts from different vantage points, which could cross in time and space. She seemed to have grasped some tendril of a very big problem—what is often referred by scholars as *polyphonics*—the interweaving of multiple perspectives on the same moment.[7] It turns out that many children think about such complex and abstract puzzles.

Daniela O'Neill, a developmental psychologist, began recording her daughter Taite's questions when Taite was just two years old. O'Neill kept the record for the following eleven years. Here is a sampling of some of the things Taite wanted to know about in the course of everyday life.

During her fourth year:
When you were small did you ever think you would drive a car or know where to go?
Where do you go when you die? Do we all die? Why do you die?
When you tweet does it give your idea to everyone at the same time?
During her fifth year:
Who made the first person before there were any people?
When I'm bigger and I know how to put myself back together again I want to open me up and see how it works.
Do you just die or do you have to do something?
Will the world ever end?
When will the world end?

What made you remember? How do you remember?
During her eighth year:
How come we have the word "awake" if we can't know if we're
not just dreaming?[8]

Though most parents don't keep records of this sort, they are in-
credibly valuable to researchers, and contain data that is very hard to
capture in a laboratory setting. Taken together, the various records that
have been kept by parents and psychologists show that children spend
most of their time on the humdrum stuff of everyday life—brushing
their teeth, finding a friend to sit near at school, watching television,
arguing, reading, playing ball, and doing chores. But that's not all they
are doing. They're also tackling some of the big conundrums of life.
Below, I describe children wrestling with three particularly knotty
problems.

The End

In 1915, my great-grandmother Annie Kramer died in her bedroom
in a house on the south fork of Long Island. Her daughter, my grandmother Helen, was seven years old and wasn't sure at first what had
happened. She had known her mother was sick, but on that day, unfamiliar adults were milling around in the small, shingled house, and
her father, who worked at a watch factory nearby, had stayed home.
An elderly woman—a great aunt, it turned out—came out of Annie's
bedroom and said to little Helen, "Your mother has gone to heaven.
Go in now and kiss her."

More than half a century later, Helen vividly recalled what happened next. She walked into the dim bedroom, where the curtains
were closed and the air smelled funny. There was her mother lying on
the bed, eyes closed. Helen felt confused. It looked to her like Annie

hadn't gone anywhere at all. But she didn't want to kiss her. She didn't know why, but her mother seemed different. Not really Annie anymore. She stood there for some minutes. Long enough, she thought, that it might seem to the people in the other room that she had drawn close to the bed, leaned down, and kissed her mother's cheek. Then she walked out of the bedroom, closing the door behind her. The elderly woman who had sent her in was standing in the parlor. "Did you kiss her, Helen?" she asked. "Did you kiss your mother goodbye?"

"Yes, I did," Helen remembered nodding.

At sixty-eight, my grandmother was heavy, lame, wrinkled, and worn. A widowed mother of two grown sons, she had lived her whole adult life on a farm, surrounded by birth and death. Reflecting on that moment that had occurred nearly sixty years before, she was uncertain. A shadow of childish worry darkened her face. She looked at me, her eight-year-old granddaughter, and admitted, "I didn't kiss her. I couldn't. I was too afraid. But I think she forgives me, don't you?"

People wrestle with the idea of death and its ramifications throughout their whole lives. For most of us, its terror and fascination cease only when death itself finally comes. But when do we *begin* thinking about it? A lot sooner than you might suspect. Children as young as two and a half begin asking how it feels to die, whether someone can return once they've died, and whether they themselves are going to die. These questions reveal their curiosity about death. But does that curiosity yield more than some bits and pieces of information? Do children actually ponder the idea of death? The sustained nature of their questioning suggests they do. Recordings of children over time show often show that they ask different questions about death on different occasions. They aren't simply perseverating, asking the same question over and over. In their somewhat sporadic way, they are exploring a big and mysterious phenomenon from different angles, trying to piece together a comprehensive understanding.

We have evidence that their efforts to gather knowledge are fruitful. As they grow, their understanding of death changes. In a series of studies, Paul Harris and his colleagues have shown that before the age of about five, children's grasp of death is rooted in the biological. They know that when something dies, it can no longer move or breathe—and that all bodily functions end They know death is *comprehensive.* They also know that once a creature dies, it cannot come back to life—death is *irrevocable.* Finally, they know that death happens to all living creatures—it is *universal.* Moreover, children have these same core insights in all cultures that have been studied.[9] It's very unlikely that all children by the time they are five have been taught those core principles of death. It's equally implausible that adults in cultures all over the world would choose to teach their children the very same things: that it shuts down all functions, is irrevocable, and happens to everyone. More likely, children's first grasp of death is based on their direct experiences with bugs and animals—and relatives.

By the time they are seven, though they continue to believe that when something dies it can no longer breathe or move, children also think that beloved pets or relatives who have died continue to have thoughts, still love them, and can see what they are doing. Rather than replacing their old intuitions with what they have heard from adults, their understanding of death comes to contain two somewhat competing orientations—one biological and the other spiritual. What might explain the inherent paradox of older children's beliefs about death? The data collected by Harris and his colleagues offers an answer. In one study, Marta Giménez and Harris provided children ages seven and eleven with one of two versions of a story. The first of them, the religious version, went like this:

> In this picture you see Sara's grandmother. At the end of her life Sara's grandmother became very ill. She was taken to a hospital

where they tried to help her but she was too old and they could not cure her. The priest came to talk to Sara about what had happened to her grandmother. He said to Sara, "Your grandmother was very ill. There is nothing the doctors could do. Your grandmother is with God now."

Then the researchers posed a series of twelve questions to each child, including "Now that Sara's grandmother is with God, do her eyes still work?" And "can Sara's grandmother still see her?"

The nonreligious version was the same, except that instead of a priest saying that Sara's grandmother was with God now, it was a doctor telling her, "Your grandmother is dead and buried now." The same questions were posed, changing only the preface from "Now that Sara's grandmother is with God . . ." to "Now that Sara's grandmother is dead and buried. . . ."

Both younger and older children seemed to understand that death entailed the end of bodily functions. One child was sure that Sara's grandmother could no longer see, explaining further that "If she is dead, nothing can work." Another responded, "He has been eaten by worms, he has no body, he just has bones." But the older children also thought that the dead person's spirit endured and had transcended the end of bodily functions. "She is still alive in the soul," one said, and another answered that "the spirit is out there and keeps feeling." Why would older children believe in something that is not supported by evidence, and couldn't possibly have revealed itself to them through personal experience? The clue comes from another feature of the study. The older children's answers were more sensitive to which story they heard. They provided more biological answers when they heard the voice of the doctor and the mention of burial, and provided more metaphysical answers when they heard the voice of the priest and the description of grandmother with God. It seems that as children acquire conventional explanations, they shift back and forth between different ideas for the same phenomena—more attuned to genre than to crafting a coherent explanation that makes sense to them.[10]

In William Faulkner's *As I Lay Dying*, Mr. Peabody says, "I can remember how when I was young I believed death to be a phenomenon of the body; now I know it to be merely a function of the mind."[11] It turns out Mr. Peabody was not alone. Most children puzzle over the vast, mysterious, and troubling nature of death and most seem to shift from a "body theory" to a "mind theory" over time. Their first intuitions are grounded in experience, their later explanations drawn from adults around them. But some will go on to acquire the intellectual tools to deliberately construct their own ideas about death, actively trying to figure out how to make sense of competing explanations. What does it look like when children do begin to piece together their own ideas? For an answer to this, we turn to another big topic that children cannot resist.

Endlessness

Two five-year-old boys who have known one another their whole lives are standing face to face on the side of a soccer field, where their older brothers are playing in a championship game. The two boys are oblivious to the game going on next to them, as well as all the other parents, grandparents, and siblings watching and shouting from the bleachers. Instead, they are locked in a mental battle. One of them says to the other, "I know everything."

"You can't know everything, Finn," the other says, flushed with emotion.

Finn, much calmer, has an air of superiority. "I do. I know everything in the universe."

"But Finn." says Rory, getting increasingly agitated, "It's not possible. You can't. No one knows everything."

"I do, though," Finn repeats. "It's true. I know everything about the whole universe."

"Finn, no one does—the universe is infinity!" Rory, his nostrils flaring, eyes wide with frustration, is now nearly beside himself. "No one can know everything about it. Infinity is way too much!"

Many young thinkers are captivated by the treacherous allure of thinking about infinity. It's extraordinarily difficult to capture these musings, however, since they usually happen when children are out of earshot, or thinking quietly to themselves. One imperfect source of data comes from adults, who often recall their childhood preoccupations. The younger the adult, the more likely their memories are to be accurate and unvarnished. They've had fewer years to rework the memory to fit their self-concept.

College students are a good source for these kinds of recollections. Consider the following, a story told to me by a nineteen-year-old student, Jonah, who had grown up in New York City. Jonah was tall with a scruffy beard and a head of brown curls. He had a habit of laughing quietly just before speaking. "When I was in kindergarten, I would mostly keep to myself," he told me. "I was one of the younger kids in the class, and shy. I was still two years out from the day when I would finally learn to read." He continued:

There was one debate, however, that really interested me and that I remember to this day. The debate was raised to me by one of my classmates—I have no idea who—and as far as I know, the teacher never weighed in on the issue. Someone asked, "Is infinity a number?" I remember thinking it must be. These were my reasons:

1. A number is something we use to represent a quantity;
2. The symbol [for infinity] represents infinity;
3. Infinity is a quantity—the biggest one there is;
4. So, infinity must be a number.

The other insight I had in kindergarten was that there *is* no highest number. I even thought of the proof:

1. Anytime someone thinks of the highest number, whether it's 1,000 or 400,000,000, you can always write 1,000 + 1, or 400,000,000 + 1.
2. That was my proof—there is no highest number because you can always just add one!

That's all I remember from five. But then, when I was in second grade, I was waiting for an elevator in some lobby with my mother—I really have no idea where, but it was in New York. In this lobby there were two opposing mirrors on the wall, and each mirror reflected the other. My mom asked me if I knew what that was called, and I said no. She said "infinity." and I felt insulted that she thought I had never heard of infinity. I had thought she was going to tell me a word for two mirrors reflecting each other.

After telling me this, Jonah left for the summer. A week later he wrote to me with more:

In eighth grade, my thoughts again turned to infinity as I became obsessed with the question "Where is the universe?" By which I meant, does the universe go on forever? How could that be? If the universe ends, and I thought it must, what is beyond the universe? Where is the universe?! This question and other related ones (Does time have a beginning and an end?) plagued me, but nobody had an answer. I remember one of my teachers when I asked him said "Jonah, there was a time when I was in college when I started thinking about those questions. I sat down and cried." But he didn't say anything more than that. I didn't really understand why that made him cry.

As I continued on with school it became more and more evident that I liked math, and that math liked me. Here's the kind of thing I like to think about, now: You are standing on a gray concrete wall. The wall is maybe 20 feet wide, 50 or 60 feet tall, and infinitely long. The ends of the wall stretch far, far into the distance beyond what the eye can see. On either side of the wall are two infinitely big basins with concrete floors. You are facing one of these basins. It's filled with water. You are looking over a vast infinite ocean that grows hazy where you stare along the horizon. Behind you is an equally large, empty basin. In your hand you hold a cup. Just a normal sized cup. You walk up to the vast ocean, bend down, and scoop up a cup of water. You carry it to the empty basin and pour it down the side. When you walk back to the full basin you realize that your cup has shrunk to half the size it was initially. You pour a half cup of water into the empty basin. On your next trip, the cup is only one-third the size it started out as. As you keep transferring the water, your cup keeps getting smaller and smaller. Soon it can hold only a drop, then, eventually only one single water molecule. Soon it takes multiple trips just to transfer one single tiny water molecule out of the whole infinite ocean. If we left the story at this point, it might seem that the character will never ever be able to fill up the basin. The power of Mathematics is that it allows us to determine the answer. Math can tell us that, yes, if you keep pouring the water at this rate for an infinite amount of time, the basin will fill up. And that's how big infinity is.

Not all children who think about endlessness when they're five are still thinking about it when they're nineteen. But the chronology of Jonah's preoccupations illustrates how a child might pursue one line of thinking over many years.

Like most weighty ideas, infinity usually slips rather than marches into children's awareness. A child looks up at the sky, and asks how many stars there are. Someone older might point out to a child that the stars go on forever. That could well be the first time a three-year-old gets a glimmer of the idea that some things go on forever. The comment may surface and disappear again without much attention from anyone. But the problem almost always reappears—a day, a week, or months later. A discussion about time or space could prompt it. The conversation might unfold between siblings, friends, or with parents. It could come up once again because of the stars. But it could crop up in a completely different context—during a game of counting, or while talking about the passage of time.

Contemplating infinity is unsettling—which may explain, in part, why it's interesting to so many children. Its messy, incomplete nature renders it very different from the neat and unambiguous ideas presented to children in school. Ironically, the number line that children are taught, usually in second or third grade, offers one of the best chances to grasp the concept of infinity. And yet, the version taught in school usually gives no hint that the number line has anything to do with infinity. Watch a child use a number line to do math problems and the difference is clear. Imagine an eight-year-old child is given a number line that looks like this:

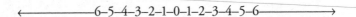

$$\longleftarrow \text{———————} 6\text{–}5\text{–}4\text{–}3\text{–}2\text{–}1\text{–}0\text{–}1\text{–}2\text{–}3\text{–}4\text{–}5\text{–}6\text{———————} \longrightarrow$$

Then they are shown an equation like this: $1+5$. Typically, they are taught to put a dot over the first numeral, in this case 1, and then advance to the right by the second numeral's number of digits or spaces, in this case 5. If they follow the procedure they have learned, they will arrive at the digit 6 and presto, they have the correct answer: $1+5=6$.

But children rarely encounter the true idea of the number line: that between every two digits there is an infinite quantity of points. Most mathematicians and educational psychologists agree that this misteaching keeps children from grasping an important concept in mathematics. As a result, they claim, children are hampered when it comes to more complex mathematics courses. It's all the more unfortunate because this important idea embedded in the number line is one that is deeply interesting to most young thinkers. What a lost opportunity.

What would happen if, instead, adults were to invite children to think out loud about infinity itself? To explore this question, Paolo Boero, Nadia Douek, and Rossella Garuti arranged for children in three fifth-grade classrooms to discuss infinity. The teachers in all three groups were trained to guide children through a series of conversations about infinity. These discussions took place over a number of days. The children were not encouraged to define infinity right away. Instead, they were encouraged to explore the idea, by saying out loud what they didn't understand and making connections between the problems of infinity and other conundrums to which they had given some thought. They were encouraged to think about infinity slowly and somewhat methodically—not to rush to a neat "solution." The children's comments show that they had increasingly accurate insights. For instance, one little boy began by saying infinity meant there was no last number. But by the third day of discussion he realized that there is, in principle, a last number, just not enough time for anyone to get to it. The topic led to a wide range of musings and insights. One child asked, "What does it mean to say that infinite numbers exist, if we cannot count them because we must die?" Another little girl noted that "the woman's body ends, but she created another woman, and so life goes on to infinity." And another: "Numbers create other numbers, to infinity, by multiplying. Each number is finite, but an infinite list is produced." By this third day, the children had collectively considered the difference between number and quantity, the relationship between infinite quantities and infinite time, and the role of an individual's finite life in the infinity of life across all people.[12]

In another study, Inger Wistedt and Mats Martinsson recorded eleven-year-old children as they worked together in groups of three on a math problem; it required them to figure out how a plank of wood of a certain length should be divided into different pieces to make three bookshelves. Because the researchers and the children had already interacted as part of a larger project focused on teaching children to think philosophically, the children were accustomed to solving unusual tasks and talking out loud about their thought processes. The transcripts show that, as the children discussed ways of dividing the wood, they spontaneously hit upon several of the trickiest aspects of thinking about infinity. At one point, a girl named Maria tried to use what she knew about dividing other discrete objects, such as apples, to solving this problem. She imagined her group trying to divide one hundred apples among the three of them: "We will get thirty-three apples each, and one apple remains. Then we divide that one. I'll get a third, and the two of you will get a third each. It can be done. Thirty-three and one third, plus thirty-three and one third, plus thirty-three and one third equals one hundred, exactly." But when she tries to use the same method to calculate on paper, it doesn't work. "I don't understand a thing!" she says. "Why could it be done a minute ago and not when you write it with numbers instead of apples?" She goes on to try and explain her own confusion: "It's because you only divide one. The numbers think that's queer and they just don't care to learn how it's done."[13]

The record of Maria's thinking shows that, in working on the problem, she put her finger on a significant mathematical issue: the difference between the infinite possible number of a class of objects, and the infinity found in something that is continuous—in this case, the piece of wood. The children used the collaborative nature of the task to trade interpretations, which allowed them to pool their knowledge, extending everyone's understanding. The researchers argue that for children to understand an enormous and difficult concept such as infinity they must actively construct, rather than simply absorb, the idea. Most children do not participate in guided discussions resembling those described in Boero's work. The vast majority of children tangle with infinity only fleetingly, pausing to mull it over now and then when playing with a friend or looking up at a starry sky. Only some will take those flashes and filaments of thought and weave them together into something more systematic and thorough when they are older.

About fifteen years after Jonah first grappled with the idea of infinity, he sat in a seminar room with me at college. This was before I knew him, before I had heard his childhood recollections. At my request, the students were, one by one, telling the group something they frequently daydreamed about. One student talked about the routes she took for her daily run. Another said she often found herself musing over the way other people interacted with one another. A third, a varsity athlete, said he fantasized about basketball. When it was Jonah's turn, he said, without pause, "I daydream about Algebra." He's headed now to graduate school in mathematics.

So far, I've discussed ideas that begin with palpable puzzles—death and infinity first appear in fairly graspable ways, and they both concern the physical world. But what about the wide universe of puzzles that emanate from the social and psychological worlds? How do children first come to think about those kinds of conundrums?

Goodness

Some of the problems that beckon children are more evanescent and intangible than death, which you can see, smell, and feel, or infinity, which gives a hint of itself through stars, counting, and the sky. When my sister Kathy was eleven years old and in sixth grade, she had a gym teacher named Miss Cooke. One day, Miss Cooke flew into a temper at a girl in Kathy's class for no apparent reason. Red-faced with fury, and with no provocation that Kathy could see, Miss Cooke charged over to the slender eleven-year-old, slammed her up against the gym wall, and yelled at her that she'd better straighten herself out.

Kathy was appalled, not just because she was unaccustomed to the violence but also because of the girl involved. She had been singled out, Kathy sensed, not because of anything she had done wrong but because she was Black. We lived on the eastern end of Long Island, where there were three groups of people who almost never crossed paths: the wealthy and privileged weekenders; the local farmers, fishermen, and tradespeople, white and mostly protestant; and the Black community, who literally lived on the other side of the railroad tracks from the whites. Many of the latter had parents or grandparents who had come to the area from the South as migrant farm workers, then chosen to stay permanently, taking year-round jobs on farms or as domestic help for wealthy white families. Our stepfather, for example, hired some of these Black men and women to work on our potato farm. Amelia, who cleaned our house and helped care for my baby sister, was Black, too. Our family had virtually no Black friends, and yet both our mother and our father (whom we visited but did not live with) talked about racism, admired the civil rights movement, and read works by Black authors.

I can only surmise the influences that led my sister to notice (and bristle at) the injustice of the racism her teacher put on crude and vicious display that day. But it didn't end there. She couldn't shake off her outrage at Miss Cooke's treatment of her fellow student. She began noticing more and mentioning it at dinnertime—I remember her asking our parents why all the Black people who worked on farms lived in a different part of town than the farms and white farmers? Sometimes she would ride along in our stepfather's pickup truck when he gave a lift at the end of the day to people who worked only during the harvest, grading potatoes. The workers would ride in the back of the truck, and my stepfather would let them off at the corner of the small road where many of them lived. My sister still remembers the jolt of seeing that their homes were small, run-down shacks. It had never occurred to her that the people who worked on the farm lived so differently than the others in our town.

Sometimes my sister rode on the harvester as it churned up potatoes from the earth. My stepfather would drive, and others, including migrant workers, would ride on the back or walk alongside, grabbing potatoes as they dropped onto a conveyer belt, where they were sorted by hand, according to their size. There was only one woman among the graders—her name was Geraldine. She seemed old to us then, though perhaps she was no more than forty. She wore old-fashioned head wraps and smoked a pipe. My sister had never before seen a woman smoke a pipe. She wanted to know Geraldine, whereas the rest of us were happy just to know *about* her. Kathy would climb down from her perch high on the harvester's side to stand next to Geraldine and help sort the potatoes. They'd chat for hours. When Kathy was twelve, she remembers, she went to a local dance at the community center. Some of the other kids at the party, who were Black, told her, "You don't dance like a white girl." My sister had no idea what they were talking about. But she wanted to.

She grew closer and closer to Amelia—a woman who dazzled with her beauty and charm. When my sister got home from school, she'd sit in the kitchen and talk for hours with Amelia. They'd go into my sister's bedroom and listen to the exciting new band, the Supremes, and practice dances like the Hitchhike. Our biological father gave her a copy of the book *Black Like Me*. She read it in one night. I was three years younger and so I must have missed a lot of the nuances of what was going on. But I could tell that she was disturbed—she was beginning to put together what had happened in school with what she saw all around her. Once she heard the word *racism*, what had begun as a mere reaction began to crystallize into something more formal. It took her a while to realize she wasn't the only one with that same idea.

It was more than sixty years ago that Lawrence Kohlberg began to explore the stages by which people arrive at what we think of as mature morality. How is it, he wondered, that nearly all two-year-olds, even the kindest and sweetest, will push, grab, and hit to fill their own needs and desires, but that by late adolescence, most children draw on a fairly abstract set of rules about right and wrong? Attempting to map that mental journey, Kohlberg began presenting children of all ages with moral dilemmas. The most famous of these is his story of Heinz, who breaks into a drugstore to steal medicine which might save his wife's life but which the druggist has priced higher than the amount of money Heinz has or can borrow. After presenting this dilemma,

Kohlberg asked each child what Heinz should do, and why. Kohlberg found that, in their earliest stage of moral development, children reason in terms of stated rules, the need for obedience, and the threat of punishment. In their elementary school years, however, children learn to think about individuals' conflicting interests, and then in terms of conventional morality—conforming with society's general views on what constitutes a good motive. According to Kohlberg, it's only at a sixth stage of moral development that people arrive at a "postconventional morality" based on considered principles of right and wrong, and children only begin exploring that territory in adolescence.[14]

For many years, Kohlberg's was the defining model of how children acquired a mature moral sense. However, over time, psychologists began to realize that what a child (or an adult, for that matter) *said* about right and wrong might not tell you much at all about what they would *do* if faced with a situation that called upon their morality. So, researchers began to devise experiments that created real dilemmas for the subjects themselves. These allowed them to watch children contend with actual situations where the decision they *should* make might be different from the one they *wanted* to. One version of this line of inquiry is the "Inequity Game" designed by Peter Blake and Katherine McAuliffe. In it, a child sits across the table from a peer. Between the children is an apparatus containing two small trays, one on either side, in which researchers visibly place M&Ms candies. The child who is actually the subject (the decider) will get to choose between two levers to pull in multiple rounds. The green lever causes the trays' contents to dump to the table allowing each child to eat whatever candy is theirs. The red lever causes the trays to empty into a middle container, to which neither child has access. Across twelve rounds, the decider is confronted with three situations: sometimes, both children are allotted the same number of candies; sometimes, the decider is allotted more candies than the other child; and sometimes, the other child is allotted more than the decider. What patterns will emerge in the decisions? If the green lever is pulled only when the amounts are the same, it suggests the subject is deciding based on a particular model of justice. If that lever gets pulled when it will dispense fewer to the decider than the peer, the subject has another model. And any deciders showing much greater tendency to pull the green lever when it will yield more candies to themselves are acting according to a very different moral compass.[15]

Repeated studies along these lines show that it's only by about age nine that children reliably reject candy when it means they arbitrarily get more than another child. Younger than that, a child is as likely as not to take whatever candy they can. They pull green levers regardless of whether the amounts are equal or greatly unequal. But other studies show that, even in these early years, the first inklings of distributive justice are emerging.

Alessandra Geraci and Luca Surian showed ten- and sixteen-month-old babies a series of four very short and quite similar animations, and tracked their eye movements as they watched. In each animation, an animal (in two segments a lion, the other two segments a bear) has two colorful discs to give out. A donkey and a cow enter the scene as the possible recipients of these treats. A chicken stays off to the side, viewing what happens, just as the baby is watching. Across the four segments, the lion always behaves differently than the bear. One distributes the discs equally to the donkey and the cow, but the other gives both the discs to just one recipient. The babies then watch a final segment in which the chicken hops through a tunnel which comes to a fork, allowing it to approach either the lion or the bear—confronting either the egalitarian or the nonegalitarian standing at a tunnel exit.

The eye-tracking would reveal which approach held more appeal for the babies. Among the ten-month-old group there was no pattern of response. These younger babies seemed to look equally whether the chicken approached the fair or unfair animal. Being an equal distributor didn't appear to register with them one way or another. However, six months is a long period of time in the life of an infant. The sixteen-month-olds spent significantly more time watching when the chicken approached the fair distributor (whether it happened to be the lion or the bear). Their steady gaze suggested that it made more sense to them. By the time children are learning to walk, they are also learning what it means to be fair.

But here we come to a bit of irony. Kohlberg's research was, quite rightly, criticized for taking children's answers to hypothetical dilemmas as evidence of their morality. It failed to distinguish between moral reasoning and moral behavior. Yet, in reaction to that flaw, researchers have gone too far in the other direction. When they measure only what children *do* when faced with ethical dilemmas, they overlook the enormous value of hearing what children *think* about morality itself. Surely, children's actions, which morph and change with development, are in part guided by their ideas about moral dilemmas. And surely, too, their thoughts are more than merely a means of assessing their cognitive abilities, as Kohlberg's model implies. Their thoughts also constitute a central part of their mental lives.

Newer research suggests ways in which this might play out. In a 2013 study, Craig Smith, Peter Blake, and Paul Harris gave children between the ages of three and eight sets of especially nice stickers—the scratch-and-sniff kind, and in their favorite colors. They, too, wanted to measure levels of sharing. They, too, used an apparatus that had trays of treats and could be manipulated to dump the treats either in the middle or in front of one of the children. But these researchers added an important twist. Before the subjects had a chance to pull any levers, each was asked to say what others should do, or to say what they themselves should do. Even the youngest children said that they and others should share and share equally—although they (accurately) predicted they would fall short of this standard in practice. The older children were much more consistent and robust in advocating for greater equity, in action as well as words.[16]

In another demonstration of this, Charles Helwig and Urszula Jasiobedzka asked children between the ages of six and eleven to make judgments about whether various hypothetical laws achieved a fair balance between individual rights and social purposes, and to explain their thinking. Among these were laws relating to traffic and vehicle use, compulsory vaccinations, and compulsory education. There were also scenarios about manifestly unjust laws, such as an imaginary land where everyone in government had green eyes, and they passed a law forbidding the teaching of math to blue-eyed children. Other discriminatory laws included one passed by rich people to deny medical care to poor people, and one created by the elderly people in a city's government making it unlawful for any young person to sit down on a bus or subway train. Asked to weigh in on such legislation, children displayed reasoning far more sophisticated than previous research had shown, very often justifying their rejection of the discriminatory laws on the basis of fairness and equality. Denying people access to education based on a trait like eye color was not only a problem because it would limit their knowledge. It was intolerable because "you're still human, you're still the same person" and "everyone should be treated equally."[17] The evidence suggests that children are thinking about these complex issues, even when they cannot offer polished answers, and even when their thoughts are imperfect blueprints for how they will act.

This isn't to say that children everywhere are thinking along identical lines. In a closely related study, Marie Schäfer, Daniel Haun, and

Michael Tomasello had children in three very different cultures—Germany, the Samburu society in rural Kenya, and the ≠Akhoe Hai‖om society in Namibia—perform a similar task. Pairs of children played a game that involved fishing cubes out of a bin. But the game was rigged so that, for half the pairs in each culture, one child was more successful than her partner in fishing out cubes. At the end of the game, each pair was given one tub of small prizes with the explanation that it contained a number of prizes equal to all the cubes the two of them had fished out. Then the experimenter left them to do what they wanted with their combined winnings.

The researchers predicted that children from Germany would tend to take a merit-based approach, so that a pair who had caught equal amounts of cubes would divide the prizes equally, but a pair with unequal success would divvy up the prizes according to their respective catches. And they predicted that the Samburu and Hai children, raised in societies that were gerontocratic and egalitarian, respectively, would tend to divide the haul equally regardless of how many cubes each child had "fished." Those predictions proved accurate. The study concludes that children's ideas about what constitutes distributive justice differ from culture to culture—but at the same time, these findings suggest a kind of universality. Children everywhere use their ideas about sharing to guide what they do.[18]

Taken together, these studies show that children's ideas about fairness matter more as they get older, that they increasingly guide children's behavior, and that those ideas incorporate a child's understanding of group norms. There may always be a gap between what people think is right and what they do in the face of temptation (think here of Anthony Weiner, Eric Schneiderman, or Eliot Spitzer as stunning examples of dissonance between explicitly stated values and behavior), but even in childhood, children's ideas play an important role in shaping their actions. We have some evidence that children weave together ideas from across many situations. In his classic book, *The Moral Child* (2008), William Damon gives a vivid example. A group of children are sitting in a pizza parlor in Worcester, Massachusetts. They are trying to figure out how to divide up a pizza.

> Child 1: Hey, there's eight pieces here. What about the extra piece?
> Child 2: The guy who's the oldest should get it. How old are you?
> Child 1: Nine.
> Child 3: I'm nine and a quarter.
> Child 1: My birthday's coming up this summer. I'm—I'll be ten in one, two months.
> Child 2 (to Child 4): How old are you?
> Child 4: Eleven, and I'll be twelve next month.
> Child 2: Well, I'm twelve, so I'll get the extra piece.
> Child 1: What about giving it to the one with the small piece?
> Child 4: Well, who's got the smallest piece?
> Child 1: I've got the smallest piece—look at it!
> Child 2: C'mon, let's cut it. The oldest kid will get one piece and the kid with the smallest piece will get one piece."

If children can so quickly and readily debate the distributive justice of sharing a pizza, you can be sure that they have each been thinking about it individually. Just as important, they are using their conversation and time together to explore the idea further. Damon points out that one feature remarkably absent from the children's musings is any consideration of what adults would think they should do.[19] In Kohlberg's terms, their ideas may have mainly reflected group norms, as expected at this age, but they were beyond a simple morality focused on avoidance of punishment or bows to authority. They were exploring their own ideas, not affirming other people's rules.

My sister's early preoccupation with racial injustice didn't fade away. She read books, talked to others interested in the same thing, and began building a deliberately diverse network of friends. She started to comprehend bigotry as a problem that extended far beyond her hometown, one that shaped economic and social structures, not just the views of individuals. Her frame of reference and her political vocabulary expanded. By the time she was fourteen, it had become a central focus of her thinking. After college she went to work full-time as an advocate for racial justice. She named her first child after two women who were Black icons—activist Ella Baker and singer Nina Simone. What began as a vague and somewhat upsetting observation percolated, collecting information and structure, until my sister had an idea that would shape her whole life.

It would be easy to interpret a particular portrait as an unusual instance—one of those singular children pursuing ambitious ideas related to infinity, mortality, or justice. Nothing could be further from the truth. Children are drawn to intellectual puzzles, and come equipped with the means to pursue such puzzles at length, and in depth. But the intellectual work they do to solve those puzzles can seem incomplete, sporadic, and inconsistent. Take Ben, for example.

The Flux and Flow of Intellectual Work

Ben was a tumultuous little boy. He was the youngest of three in an energetic and voluble family. So the intensity of Ben's feelings, and the power with which he expressed them, ensured that he held his own with his older sister and brother. When upset, the corners of his wide, mobile mouth would turn down, his lips darken with emotion. In those moments, it looked like someone had drawn his features on his face with a crayon. A deep flush would spread across his cheeks, high up just under his eyes. In an instant he could look like someone who hadn't slept in days, or had spent too much time in a chlorinated pool. But he was tough, which meant that he seemed outraged just as often as miserable. He'd shout while he cried—furious that no one was listening to him at the dinner table, distraught that he had lost in the ping-pong tournament his extended family held every August, angry that his sister had teased him, frustrated that the family had chosen the movie the others wanted, not the one he had championed.

Ben had a big vocabulary, and a taste for the crowd. Often at family gatherings he wanted to make a toast. He'd use phrases that seemed strange coming from an eight-year-old. Ending each sentence with a question mark, he'd begin: I'd like to thank my family? For supporting me all these years? And I wish everyone a very merry Christmas? I'd also like to thank Mr. Claus? He has a lot of places to go tonight, and I'm so grateful he's coming here. And Santa? I'd really love a new pair of ice skates? And an iPhone? And anything you have from Spider-Man!" He'd sink back in his chair, relieved and delighted to have had his moment in the limelight, and to have said his piece. But he wasn't on stage most of the time. More often he was busy throwing himself into some game or scenario, charging around transforming pillows and blankets into shelters for his superheroes, laying out scripts for his friends to join in, giving all he had to complex and exhausting games of catch with his brother. His joy was as intense as his despair.

To his parents, during his ninth summer, he seemed particularly volatile. He complained a lot as they embarked on their annual road trip from the west coast to the east, visiting various family and friends along the way. He wanted cucumbers and soy sauce, his favorite. No more weird vegetables, no more hot dogs. He hated having to share a bed with his brother. Why couldn't he have his own bed? He missed his best friend. He didn't want to go hiking every day like the others in the family.

One night, while visiting cousins, he became particularly riled up. His birthday was just two days away and, with characteristic passion, he was simultaneously beside himself with excitement and over-wrought with anxiety. What if the celebration wasn't what he had dreamed of? What if he didn't get good presents? How sad would he be at the end of the day when his birthday was over? Bedtime just intensified this storm of feelings. He began sobbing, his small shoulders shaking, tears and drool pooling together on his chin and on his mother's shoulder.

"What is it, Ben?" his mother asked. "What is making you so sad?"

"I feel terrible," he moaned. "It's just everything. I don't know what I'm good at. I don't even know what I'm going to do when I grow up. What if I never get a profession? What if I can't earn a living? I don't even know what acid is."

"Acid?" his mother repeated, confused.

"Yeah, I don't even understand what it is."

Bewildered as to what Ben was talking about, his mother hugged him and rubbed his back until he calmed down. Eventually Ben fell asleep. Relieved that the storm had passed, Ben's mother put it out of her mind.

A few days later, Ben and his older cousin Isaac, a chemistry major in college, were sitting at the kitchen table together, eating brownies. They had been talking about a comic book in which the villain threw acid at the superhero. Ben looked up, his mouth bulging with brownie. "I was just wondering. What *is* acid?"

Isaac looked back blankly. "What?"

"I don't get what is acid," Ben persisted. "Is all acid the same?"

Isaac wasn't sure what Ben was getting at. But he did know how to explain acid, so he happily launched into a description of the chemical structure of acid. Ben stopped chewing. He sat there, eyes glued to his cousin's mouth, determined not to miss one word.

Isaac only realized the heart of the matter a few days later, when Ben returned to the topic. Ben's mother was making salad dressing. She tasted it, and then added a little lemon juice. Ben was watching her. "So, acid's good. But it's bad sometimes? So it's food, *and* it's a weapon?"

"I guess," his mother said, and turned back to her cooking.

Later that night, Isaac said to his aunt, "I know what's on Ben's mind. He's trying to figure out what makes acid acid. Like Aristotle's 'natural kinds,' you know?"

Ben was tussling with a very big problem: What gives something its identity? It wasn't yet a formal idea for him—but he was working on it. There was one more intellectual tool Ben needed to pursue his ideas in the way that Isaac did. He had to learn how to treat his ideas like objects.

Children Think about Ideas

Jean Piaget was the first psychologist who tried to identify developmental patterns in children's ideas. His method was simple, yet extraordinarily innovative. He simply asked young children how they explained various complex and mysterious phenomena. He asked for their thoughts on topics like animacy, dreaming, and the cause of seasons, to name a few. Here is an example of his questions to a six-year-old about the nature of animacy:

E: Is a lizard alive?
C: Yes.
E: A nail?
C: No.

E: Is the sun alive?

C: Yes.

E: Why?

C: Because it moves when it has to.[20]

He was the first great sleuth of children's minds. He dared to ask children their thoughts and assumed that their answers could tell us something about how they made sense of the world. But his approach was even more avant-garde than that. He expected even four- and five-year-old children to consider big ideas. He assumed that, even if the answers were wrong by conventional adult standards, those initial attempts at mentally organizing the world were vital to the process of acquiring more accurate or powerful thoughts. [21]

But Piaget's method (like everyone else's) constrained what he could discover. By using such a tight question-and-answer format, which had a strong feeling of "quiz" to it, he signaled to children that they should respond with what they knew, not take the opportunity to explore an interesting topic. In his effort not to affect what they said, he robbed the conversations of certain characteristics children require to reveal their best thinking. He ended up with a picture (and a somewhat impoverished one at that) of their knowledge, rather than their ideas.

Research has shown that children are surprisingly sensitive to the epistemological nature of a given exchange. They are alert to cues that tell them when another person is trying to share an idea with them (as opposed to, say, a funny story, or a practical piece of information). When Lucas Butler and Ellen Markman showed three- and four-year-old children a small object they had never seen before, which they called a blicket, all of the children observed that blickets were, among other things, magnetic. But they encountered this information in three different ways. One group of children watched as the blicket accidentally magnetically attracted a paper clip, while the adult was handling it. A second group had it explained to them by an experimenter that the blicket could be used as a magnet. A third group of children saw the adult deliberately use the blicket to lift paper clips magnetically, although the adult neither said nor did anything to indicate she was trying to teach the children that the blicket was magnetic. Soon after seeing one of these demonstrations, each child was given some blickets that, unbeknownst to them, were not magnetic. This gave the researchers a chance to see how long each child would persist in trying to use a blicket as a magnet—a sign that they had generalized the property of magnetization from their initial encounter. The researchers reasoned that the longer a child persisted, the more fully that child had internalized the idea that blickets are magnetic. Three-year-old children who had seen an adult deliberately use a blicket as a magnet kept trying to use the new, nonmagnetic blicket to lift a paper clip. It didn't matter whether an adult had been trying to teach them about blickets or not. In contrast, only the four-year-olds who had been explicitly taught that blickets were magnetic persisted in trying to get the new blickets to attract a paper clip. Butler and Markman argue that, between the ages of three and four, children begin to decipher something important about the role of humans in shaping and communicating ideas. By four years of age, but not before, they distinguish between someone's intention toward an object and the intention to share an idea. Children not only learn the content of other people's ideas this way, they learn that ideas are made by and exchanged between people.[22] Piaget's young subjects may have been trying to tell him the same thing.

Nearly one hundred years later, Nilkos Pramling reanalyzed Piaget's old data asking children what they thought about lizards, planets, dreams, and the nature of causality. By looking much more closely at the answers themselves (rather than at Piaget's coding of those answers), Pramling found evidence that the children were more sophisticated than Piaget had thought. Where Piaget had seen evidence of overly concrete and illogical thinking (for instance, describing a dream as something that happens in front of one's eyes), Pramling found that, actually, children had been struggling to convey elusive and complex phenomena. One of Piaget's young subjects had even said, "It's as if it were happening in front of your eyes." Far from having a primitive or naive way of thinking about dreams, the child was trying to convey the paradox that dreams are not material, but feel vivid.[23] Perhaps Piaget's young subjects had a subtler, more advanced grasp of what it takes to explore a complex or abstract phenomenon than he realized.

Piaget's missteps are suggestive in other ways, as well. To come up with a new idea, or truly consider someone else's, at some point in development children need to recognize that they are doing so. Aristotle believed the mark of an educated mind was the ability to consider an idea fully, without embracing it. Very young children do not treat an idea as an object one can step away from, look at from several angles, or revisit. It takes time and education to do so—and for that to occur, children first need to acquire an idea about ideas. When does this happen?

To answer this question, my students and I asked four- and six-year-old children to tell us what an idea was. Then we asked them to tell us one of their ideas. Below are some of their answers.

> Child: You could make anything you want, if you have one.
> Experimenter: So, what is your idea?
> Child: To make a knot and it close.

> Experimenter: So, what was your idea?
> Child: I don't know, I forgot it at home!

Ideas

Experimenter: What did you forget at home?
Child: My idea!

Experimenter: So, I'm wondering what an idea is.
Child: Oh, an idea is something that you think!
Experimenter: It's something that you think?
Child: It's amazing, or it can be kind of scary.
Experimenter: It's amazing? Why's that?
Child: Because it matters—because, it's kind of like. So, like, you might think of bad stuff.

Experimenter: Can you give me an example of an idea that you've had? Or that you've heard? It could be anything.
Child: My idea was to get a guinea pig!

Child: Um, something that like, that you want to be true kind of, or they couldn't be true, that like . . .

Experimenter: It depends?
Child: Yeah, and, like, you think of them in your mind.
Experimenter: In your mind?
Child: Or you can see them, like with your eyes.
Experimenter: How do you see them?
Child: If I saw a rope ladder, then maybe I would think I could build a tree house.

Child: An idea is something what you think about, that you think will work. Like if you're trying to jump over a swing, you get an idea.
Experimenter: And what if it doesn't work?

Child: If it doesn't work, you don't make an idea, you didn't make an idea.

These data suggest that younger children think of an idea as a plan or as a concrete object that reflects their thoughts (a drawing, for instance). But by the time they are six, more of them think that an idea is a conceptual object. They understand that ideas can be good or bad. At about this same time, children not only can explore an idea with a certain degree of Aristotelian detachment, they like to.

In the early 1980s, philosopher Gareth Matthews began talking to children about philosophy. Though not interested in conducting traditional psychological experiments, he *was* interested in finding out if children could think about philosophical problems in a philosophical way. To find out, he'd tell a story to children about kids their age encountering a problem whose solution required philosophical reasoning. In one story, for example, two children are looking forward to seeing a historic ship they will visit on an upcoming trip. But they wonder: Since everything on it—every sail, plank, and iron fitting—has been replaced at one time or another in its preservation, is it actually still the same ship? One child says yes, the other no.

Having read one of these brief stories aloud, Matthews asked his young listeners which of the children in the story was right. Most of the stories he read did not have an ending, so he'd also invite his audience to offer the best conclusion. Children's responses to these philosophical narratives provided startling evidence that children as young as five and six were interested in such stories, and eager to think about such abstract and subtle problems. But the responses offer us another important clue. The children responded with extraordinary alacrity, jumping right into the activity and immediately bringing to bear various kinds of reasoning. This suggests that such thinking was not altogether new to them. It was a step, not a jump, from their own spontaneous forms of thought. In many cases, they seemed to have already thought about one or more aspects of the problem. Here, for example, is another of Matthews's stories:

"Hello, Freddie, how was school?" It was Freddie's mother, greeting him as he came up the garden path.

"Good," replied Freddie, "but you know, we've got this weird kid from Stornoway in my science class. He's called Ian. He whispered to me during class today, 'Cheese is made of grass.' 'You've got to be kidding,' I said. Then Mr. McColl, our teacher, noticed us talking and asked what it was all about. Ian repeated what he said to me—'Cheese is made of grass.' 'That's a very interesting bit of reasoning,' Mr. McColl said, 'we must discuss it next week.' What do you suppose he meant?"

"That's easy," said Alice, who had been eating a yogurt in the doorway and listening in on the conversation. "He means that cows make milk out of grass and farmers make cheese out of milk. If *a* is made of *b* and *b* is made of *c,* then *a* is made of *c.* Cheese is made of milk and milk is made of grass, so cheese is made of grass."

By this time Freddie had made it into his front hallway and had dropped his books onto the floor. He gave Alice a dirty look. Then he turned to his mother. "Is Alice right, Mum?" he asked.

"Let's talk about it over the dinner table," replied his mother. "I have an errand to run just now."

The children listening to the story, Matthews reports, found Alice's reasoning quite acceptable. One of them, Donald, summed it up: "In a way it's true. . . . It sounds unusual, but grass *is* cheese, in a way; it's just the first stage of what becomes cheese—the second stage is milk. . . . The third stage is cheese." Donald continued: "It's all the same thing really, just different stages as it matures." Another child noted, "We don't really notice what stuff is actually made of. . . . They have four different stomachs."

At a certain point in the session, Matthews raised the possibility that there was a difference between what something is made *from* and what it is made *of*. The children picked up this line of thinking and agreed that a book is made *of* paper. But paper, many of them said, is not really made *of* wood, though it may be made *from* wood.

"If it was made *of* wood," one ten-year-old named Martin said, "it would be, you know, *wooden*."

Matthews sums up the discussion one of his groups held: "So in the end my kids in Edinburgh . . . were willing to say that milk is made by cows *from* grass, and that cheese is made by farmers *from* milk or, perhaps, from cream. But they were inclined to deny, correctly, I should say, though they didn't ask my opinion, that cheese is made *of* milk and also deny that milk is made *of* grass."[24]

The enthusiasm with which children considered Matthews's conundrums is telling. If they can launch into such careful reasoning about something as unwieldy and perplexing as the nature of identity, it seems unlikely that this was their first attempt to think through a complex or abstract idea. Instead, his account provides support for the proposition that children ponder such matters even if they don't always share their thoughts in an obvious way.

We have since gained more systematic data showing the same thing. In their book *Children Talk about the Mind*, Karen Bartsch and Henry Wellman describe the ways in which young children use phrases like thinking, knowing, and wanting, to reveal their expanding understanding of the very idea that there is such a thing as a mind. Typically by age three, children make it clear they are spending at least some of their time thinking about thinking. Consider the exchange

Bartsch and Wellman report between Adam, just shy of three years old, and a grownup:

> Adam: I . . . just thinking?
> Adult: You're just thinking?
> Adam: Yes.
> Adult: What are you thinking about?
> Adam: Thinking 'bout leaf.[25]

Children's use of verbs like *think* shows that they have some nascent awareness that thinking is a distinct activity, something they know that they *do*, like jump or sing. One of my favorite examples of this comes from a young colleague who took her two-year-old son, Miro, to a museum. As they stood together gazing at a large, abstract painting by Picasso, Miro, elfin-like, said in his surprisingly raspy voice and rapid-fire intonation, "That's provocative."

His mother was taken aback. "It's provocative?"

Miro pointed to his head. "It makes you think."

Later, after she and I had shared a laugh about this, she explained that she and Miro did "talk about art a lot together." She concluded that this must have been a word she had used along the way:

> I think in these conversations, he came to the not-quite-right idea that "provocative" is a word that can be applied to all abstract art, no matter what. He only uses the word for art, and he uses it specifically for art that doesn't have anything else in it he'll recognize. Like, if it were a sculpture of a cat, he'd say, "That art is a cat!" And if it were a moon, he'd say, "That art is a moon!" And if it's a Picasso and it's not clearly a cat or moon, he'd say "That art is provocative!" He calls his own art provocative,

because it's scribbles. I think he thinks it means "art that is not clearly something."

We have other indirect evidence that young children are sensitive to the components of ideas. Four-year-old children seem aware that the facts they'll need to solve a problem depend on what they already know. Carolyn Baer and Ori Friedman asked four-, five-, and six-year-olds to teach a stuffed bear something new. The children were to tell the bear about a very unusual umbrella that looked just like a big green frog. In one condition, the children were told that the bear knew a lot about umbrellas, even though he had never seen an umbrella like this one. In a second condition, children were told that the bear knew nothing about umbrellas at all. The researchers were focused on how the children's use of general information (umbrellas keep you dry) versus specific information (it's green) would differ across these conditions and their different ages. Four-year-olds offered the same blend of general and specific information no matter what they had been told the bear already knew. Five-year-olds, however, used general information only when talking to the "naive" bear, and left it out, leaping to the specific information, when they were teaching an umbrella-savvy bear.[26]

In another intriguing line of research, Igo Bascandziev and Paul Harris have been probing the possibility that children engage in thought experiments as well as physical ones. In one of their studies, three- and four-year-old children watch an experimenter drop a ball into one of three cups, each of which is connected by an opaque, S-shaped tube to one of three cups below. As the ball is held above the cup where it will be dropped, the child is asked to predict in which of the lower cups it will land. In the condition of the study where they are simply looking on, three-year-olds indicate that the ball will land in the cup directly under the cup where the experimenter drops it—a simple, gravity-based deduction that misses the effect the bent tube will have. In the condition where the children are given a chance to fiddle around with the device, however, many revise their intuitive theory and predict the ball will land in the cup where the tube ends.[27]

So far, the study showed what Piaget and his many disciples have suggested—that through their own actions children will discover something new about how the world works. But Bascandziev and Harris wanted to find out whether children could also learn about the world by thinking about it. So, in another condition of their study, instead of allowing the children to touch the device, they offered them information about why and how the ball might land in a different position than where it was dropped. The effect was the same: even the three-year-olds began looking in the right place. Note that this research does not show learning due to direct instruction. It's well established by now that simply providing a child with the right answers does little to change the way the child thinks. Instead, once the children were invited to visualize various aspects of the setup, they led themselves to a new thought. Bascandziev and Harris show that even three- and four-year-olds can and do engage in deliberate thought experiments—and that such experimentation is as much a contemplative activity as it is a physical one.

Carefully constructed experiments like this one are revealing because they cause children to engage in sustained, deliberate consideration of an unfamiliar idea. At the same time, it's clear that in the course of everyday life children often don't choose to do this. It might be because not all thought experiments come dressed alike.

When Matthews invited schoolchildren to talk with him, he hit upon an important clue about the path along which children acquire the ability to delve into an idea: that path is filled with stories. Educators, like novelists, know that putting something into a story makes it more appealing, particularly to young listeners. But there's evidence to suggest that stories do more than entice; they mirror a fundamental structure of thinking. We have known for at least thirty-five years now that a story structure is children's first and most powerful way of making sense of the world around them. Children naturally organize their daily experience around a beginning, middle, and an end. They do this when they narrate factual as well as fictional events. Every story contains characters, a problem, and its resolution. Narrative structure not only helps young children make sense of their daily lives, it paves the way for more abstract kinds of thinking.

For instance, imagine a three-year-old who often goes to the zoo. She develops a script for zoos: "When we go to the zoo, I feed the sea lions, and sometimes we visit the snakes. If we have time, Dad buys me Cracker Jacks." Out of such scripts emerges children's ability to tell stories about particular experiences: "One time, we went to the zoo and the snakes were gone. So we saw the parrots." By narrating their experiences, first with scripts and then with stories, children begin to reorganize objects and events into more abstract categories. Groupings like "animals I see when I go to the zoo" eventually lead to concepts such as "wild animals," "big cats," and "mammals."

This fundamental feature of early mental development may explain why Matthews's approach seemed so fruitful. Perhaps by conveying philosophical problems in a story form, Matthews had rendered abstract ideas accessible and meaningful to young children. To find out if this might be true, Anna Deloi (now Anna Kirby) and I carried out a series of experiments with kindergarteners. In the first study, Anna told some children one of two stories about the idea of fairness. One of these stories involved characters and a situation with which we expected children to closely identify. Here's how Anna presented this first story:

I'm going to tell you part of a story and see if you can help me finish it. The story goes like this: One day, a girl named Emily was watching her favorite TV show in her living room. Her parents' friends were visiting, and they had three kids who were just around Emily's age: Tommy, Katie, and Alex. Suddenly, Tommy, Katie, and Alex ran into the living room and demanded that Emily turn off her show so that they could watch a movie instead. Emily didn't think it was fair at all because she had been there first and she wanted to watch her show just as much as they wanted to watch their movie. But the others said that what three wanted was more important than one. How do you think the story should end? (Child responds) So, that story was about fairness, which can be a confusing idea. If someone asked you what fairness means, what would you tell them?

Children in a second group heard a very similar story. This one also revolved around the idea of fairness, but depicted a farmer, and the sale of land—a unfamiliar situation and set of characters. Anna presented it as follows:

I'm going to tell you part of a story and see if you can help me finish it. The story goes like this: Years ago, there was a farmer living on a little plot of land, growing corn. A new company moved into town to build some big office buildings. One day, three of the men from the company came onto the farmer's land and demanded that he sell his farm to them and let them build a new office building there. The farmer didn't think it was fair, because he had been there first and he wanted to farm just as much as they wanted to build, but the men from the company said that what three wanted was more important than just one.

How do you think the story should end? (Child responds) So, that story was about fairness, which can be a confusing idea. So next I want to know: if someone asked you what fairness means, what would you tell them?

Children in a third condition heard an explanation of fairness rather than a story, but it was precisely comparable in vocabulary and length to the two stories above. The explanation version was the kind of very clear but prosaic explanation that teachers offer children in school about all sorts of topics. It went like this:

I'm going to tell you an idea I've been thinking about and see what you think. I've been thinking about what makes something fair. A lot of times, you hear people say that something is fair or unfair, but I'm not sure what they mean because I don't know what *I think* fair is. If something is good for some people, but bad for other people, how do you know if it's fair? Fair might always be what's good for the biggest number of people. Or maybe sometimes, what one person needs is more important than what the group needs. What do you think? Which of those sounds like the right meaning of fairness to you? (Child responds) So, that was a good conversation about fairness, but it's still a confusing idea. So next I want to know: if someone asked you what fairness means, what would you tell them?

Children who heard a story, whether about Emily or about the farmer, learned more about the concept of fairness than children who heard the explanation. Their answers were more accurate and informative. It comes as no surprise that children derived more knowledge of a concept when it was embedded in a story than they did when it was presented in a more didactic way. But because we were interested in children's eagerness to engage in ideas, we also measured the number of words they used in their answers. We reasoned that if one kind of story or explanation worked better to engage children in the consideration of ideas, that would show up as an interest in talking at greater length about the idea. Sure enough, the Emily and Farmer stories prompted longer, more detailed responses.

One possible interpretation of our data is that stories beget stories, and the greater number of words children use merely reflect their tendency to continue with the storytelling per se, rather than interest in thinking about the idea of fairness. That is not, however, what we observed. The children did not extend the story, or start a new one—they spoke more about the idea itself. The children who had heard the straightforward explanation of fairness were the ones who had the most difficult time explaining the idea.

The content of the two stories turned out to matter, as well. The children who heard about Emily provided clearer explanations and were more eager to discuss the idea of fairness than those who heard the story of the farmer. The story form, it seems, is a powerful and alluring structure for engaging with ideas, but the best stories for eliciting children's richest thinking are ones whose content and characters resonate most with their own experience.[28]

It seems clear that a well-constructed narrative increases children's willingness to engage with an idea when it's offered. But beyond that heightened interest, do narratives help children actually understand or learn a new idea? To find out, Anna and I tried two ways of introducing kindergarten and first-grade students to a challenging idea. This study had four conditions: subjects were presented with one or the other of two philosophical concepts—dualism and absolutism—and they were taught in either a pedagogical or a narrative way. For example, the children in the dualism / pedagogical condition were provided with the following explanation:

I want to tell you about a cool idea you might not know about. It's called dualism, and it's the idea that people are made up of two separate parts, a body and a mind. You know that you have a brain inside your head, right? Your brain is part of your body, and it's working all the time to control how you move around and to help your eyes and ears to recognize the things around you. But people who believe in the idea of dualism say that your *thoughts and feelings* don't come from your brain, they come from your mind, which is something that can't be seen or touched. That's why you can feel one way in your body, but totally different in your mind. Like, your body might not feel hungry at all, but your mind might still want some ice cream, right? You don't want it because your body needs food, you want it because you know in your mind that it tastes really good, or because all your friends are having it and you want to eat with them and have fun. Whenever your mind and your body say different things like that, it's an example of dualism. What do you think about that idea? Do you agree or disagree with it?

Contrast this with the experimenter's words in the dualism / narrative condition, which some other children heard:

I want to tell you a story. Once upon a time, the chef at the biggest restaurant in New York City had a birthday party. There were games, and dancing, and everyone who worked in the restaurant made the chef's favorite foods. Then, the baker brought out a beautiful, ten-layer cake. At that point, the chef felt so stuffed, he wasn't sure there was any space left in his stomach. But he knew that the cake was delicious, and he wanted some anyway. "How can I be so stuffed, but still want cake?" he asked his friend. "Well, your stomach is part of your body, and your body feels full," his friend replied, "but your mind is different from your body, and your mind is what wants cake. That's called dualism—the idea that your body and your mind are different things, so they can want and feel different things." The chef nodded his head at the idea, before devouring four slices of cake. Afterward, he felt quite sick. But he still felt happy at how much fun the party was. "I feel terrible in my body." he mused, "but my mind is happy! That sounds like dualism again!" What do you think about dualism? Do you agree with the chef's friend?

In both of these dualism-teaching conditions, the next step was to ask the child to choose the statement that best defined dualism from a set of five possibilities:

1. Your mind and your body are separate things, and sometimes they feel differently.
2. Everyone has his or her own thoughts and feelings.
3. Your brain helps you move around the world and see and feel things.
4. All the parts of you always want the same things at the same time.
5. It's sometimes really hard to make up our minds about what we want.

The child was also presented with another list of five statements and asked which sounded most like an example of dualism:

1. You're at a sleepover, and your body feels really sleepy, but your mind wants to stay awake to spend more time with your friends.

2. You stubbed your toe and now your mind can't think about anything else because your body hurts.
3. During a soccer game, you think about kicking the winning goal and then your foot does it.
4. You can't fall asleep, so you focus your mind really hard on relaxing and it helps you fall asleep faster.
5. You just ate a delicious meal of your favorite foods, and it made you feel really happy.

The result was that children learned more and had a more accurate understanding of the idea (whether dualism or absolutism) when they heard it embodied in a story.

Readers may shrug, thinking it's obvious that children would get more out of stories than they would out of abstract, logical expositions. And yet, these drier forms of explanation and definition make up most of what teachers offer to young students, whether they are trying to teach simple facts or complex concepts. Children spend most of their days following procedures and instructions on worksheets or a whiteboard, and digesting information from content-specific textbooks. It's mainly outside of school—at home, on the playground, in the grocery store—that they absorb all kinds of food for thought in the stories they overhear. Evidence suggests that all those casual narratives have an impact.

Carolyn Schult and Henry Wellman told stories to children between the ages of two and four that contained in every case some surprising turn of events. One story, for example, depicted a little boy who, having decided he would like milk with his cereal, took a pitcher from the refrigerator and proceeded to pour orange juice into the bowl instead. Then the children were asked: "Why did that happen? Why did Jimmy pour orange juice on his cereal?" Children didn't always articulate the most convincing reasons, but they did come up with causes that matched the outcomes (something Jimmy thought or felt made him use orange juice instead of milk).[29] Explaining causation was the focus of another study, too, by Wellman and his colleagues. They used the CHILDES database to analyze children's spontaneous explanations for all kinds of human actions, and found a similar ability to think through situations where relatable people were involved. Three-year-old Adam said, "I talking very quiet because I don't want somebody to wake up." Ross, age four years and eight months, said, "He'll eat his food, because to be alive." Later, Ross said, "He got a bad tooth because he fell off his bike on his face."[30] The children's statements showed that they could formulate different kinds of explanations—psychological, physical, or biological—as appropriate to different events. By three, children are, without knowing it, assembling a framework for constructing verbal theories of causation.[31]

And yet, one vital piece of the story has remained in darkness. We now know that children can explain things in more accurate and thoughtful ways than we used to believe possible. But there's a difference between what you *can* explain, and what you *want* to discover an explanation for. I have tried to show that children are beginning to form ideas when they are very young. But the story doesn't end there. While every three-year-old is a fledgling intellectual, only some will continue on that path. By late adolescence, there is a vivid difference between those who eagerly and doggedly pursue an idea, and those who don't.

By the time students are in college, many are able to learn abstract concepts and the outlines of complex ideas. They probably had to in high school, where they may have been asked to explain the roots of the French Revolution, define inert matter, or critique the idea of capitalism. They can study ideas, but that doesn't mean they actively pursue their own. By early adulthood, few will eagerly hone a new idea, gather fresh knowledge to improve it, or revisit it from different angles in order to strengthen it. As children grow, they may have a thousand and one ideas, but many never go beyond those fleeting, flimsy, often ordinary small ideas. They haven't made the connection between the small ideas of daily experience and the big ones that shape their lives and might affect the lives of others.

Freud's Ghost

Tony Greenwald's scientific breakthrough didn't feel earth-shattering. It didn't even feel all that new. It just seemed to him that he and his colleague Mahzarin Banaji, working together at the University of Washington, had noodled their way from some psychological experiments they admired to a cool new research method.

In 1980, Greenwald had published an important and influential paper called "The Totalitarian Ego." In it he argued that a person's sense of self dictated what that person remembered about his or her life.[32] His argument took hold: researchers everywhere were talking about it and designing experiments to test it. But Greenwald's interests were not static. As scientists tend to do, he shifted the focus of his experiments over time. Often, one study would open up an unexpected path to another, moving him toward a new topic. By 1990, most of his publications focused on people's attitudes. He, like many social psychologists of the day, wanted to know why people so stubbornly hold on to certain attitudes, and what conditions might make people more open to changing their minds. The focus of his experiments had shifted, but his intellectual commitments had not. All along he was interested in how people's thoughts and behaviors are governed by an internal boss, one who was hard to pin down but seemed to rule with an iron fist.

Greenwald also began an additional line of inquiry. He was interested in the kinds of categories people unknowingly applied to matters requiring judgment. He wanted to know why it was so easy to predict which of two candidates, one male and one female, would get a job offer and why white customers were so much more likely to approach a white salesman over a Black one. He knew that if you asked people whether a man was more qualified than a woman for an important job, experimental participants would insist gender had nothing to do with it. Similarly, if you asked white people whether they believed white people made better salespeople, they would deny it. Greenwald knew that the mismatch between what people said about their attitudes, and how they behaved was not just a small wrinkle, or a glitch, it was a feature of a vast and important psychological phenomenon. It was Narnia's wardrobe.

Meanwhile, like psychologists across the country, Greenwald was headily exploring how computers could offer powerful new ways to peek into people's minds and spot tendencies they themselves would or could not report. The method he hit upon only seemed obvious once he had devised it. It went like this: If people regularly link certain categories together (male and competent, for instance), words that conjure those categories should be easier to match up than words from two categories people don't usually associate with one another (for instance, female and competent, or male and incompetent). Using a simple software application, you could ask hundreds of people to engage in a quick word-sorting game and capture their clicks. In a way a human researcher could not, the computer could detect tiny differences in response time as subjects encountered words from categories they usually did or did not associate with one another.

To test the concept, Greenwald and Banaji first created a computer-based exercise featuring names of insects and flowers, as well as some things most people find pleasant (such as *gentle, heaven, friend*) and some things most people regard as unpleasant (such as *danger, vomit, gloom*). Subjects sat before a screen on which two columns were displayed, and they were given the following instructions: The screen is going to show you fifty-eight words, one at a time. For every word that is *either* a flower or something pleasant to you, click the button on your left. For every word that is *either* an insect or something un-pleasant to you, click the button on your right.

Greenwald and Banaji timed how long each person took to assign the whole list of words to either the left- or the right-hand column. Then they gave subjects a second list. This list also contained words that were either insects or flowers, pleasant or un. But this time, sub-jects were asked to put all the pleasant words and insects to the left, and all the unpleasant words and flowers to the right. They reasoned that if people resisted associating insects with pleasant things, and flowers with unpleasant things, this version of the game should take people longer to play. That is exactly what happened.[33]

Having discovered that the time people take to assign words to a column is a reliable measure of their implicit associations, Greenwald and Banaji were ready to measure what they really cared about: racial bias. In the second version of the test, they asked people to look at pictures of people and words that might have negative or positive as-sociations for them. So, for instance, a subject might see twenty-eight items, half of which were images of Black or white children's faces, and half of which were words like *lucky, peace, sincere,* and *sweet,* as well as *hatred, agony, rotten,* and *tragedy.* After Greenwald had pro-grammed the computer so that the words and images were presented quickly (so quickly that the subject had no time to edit his or her thoughts) he took the test. Even he, who had developed the theory of implicit associations and designed the study, took more time when he completed the version in which negative words were matched with the faces of white people, and positive words were matched with the faces of Black people.

Aghast at his own performance on the task and what it said about his own implicit bias, Greenwald was at the same time thrilled by the power of his method. He knew he was on to something important. But he didn't immediately realize just how his technique would reverberate throughout the field of psychology. Within a few years, the Implicit Associations Test had become an essential item in the researcher's toolkit, allowing psychologists to peer into the shadowy recesses of people's minds to see how they organized their daily experiences. It has been used in other ways to gauge people's unconscious racism, but also to reveal other hidden biases associated with age, sex, athletics, and religious affiliations. It is even used to measure people's views of themselves.[34] In one study, Marlene Sandstrom and Rachel Jordan used the test to measure children's self-esteem, having found that confident children take less time to sort words about themselves on the same side as positive phrases. Children with negative opinions about themselves do just the opposite.[35] Greenwald and Banaji seem to have given us an X-ray machine for thinking.

Just as importantly, Greenwald and Banaji's research spread out far beyond laboratories. Their conclusions transformed the way modern society thought about racism. Until then, there was a commonly held belief, at least in the United States, that we know our own opinions and points of view: if a person said she wasn't racist then she wasn't racist, and if a person behaved in a racist way, it was expected that she'd admit it. What you said was what you thought. And what you thought you thought could be trusted. Tony Greenwald showed us how wrong that belief was. Even he, who studied the phenomenon, hadn't been able to identify his own thoughts, buried deep within his mind.

Within ten years of the first use of the Implicit Associations Test, the idea of implicit bias had filtered into the public consciousness, and become part of conversations all over the country. No longer an eso-teric concept researched by academics, it was a term on everyone's lips. In 2016, during the first US presidential debate of that election year, the democratic nominee Hillary Clinton said, "implicit bias is a problem for everyone, not just police."[36]

In April 2018, two men who were Black walked into a Starbucks in Philadelphia and sat down at one of the tables, but did not order anything. Within moments, a white employee had called the police, who came and arrested the men for loitering. But prosecutors declined to press charges, because there was no evidence that either of the men had committed any crime. The misdeed, it seemed, was not committed by either of the men, who had simply been looking for a friend, but by the employee who had jumped to the wrong conclusion—that a Black man who had not yet bought a coffee must be looking for trouble. The employee was fired, and Starbucks CEO Kevin Johnson admitted that even a business with a progressive reputation can harbor "unconscious bias." He announced that the chain would close all eight thousand of its shops for one day in order to provide its 175,000 employees with anti-bias training. In just twenty years, a simple test that anyone could take in a just a few minutes had led to a sea change in how society talked about racism. Tony Greenwald's idea had become ubiquitous. In fact, by 2018 it was so recognizable, Starbucks trusted it enough to forfeit millions of dollars in revenue in order to mend their reputation.

The core of their theory, however, was not new. It had been lin-gering in the ether for well over a century, since its beginnings in mid-nineteenth-century Vienna, when Freud developed the idea of un-conscious. Freud's theory is a perfect example of an idea that can retain its deep influence even as it is roundly rejected. It isn't only that Freud is regularly discarded by psychology departments; the broader rejec-tion comes from the general population, only a tiny minority of which is willing to acknowledge that they have thoughts and feelings of which they are unaware.[37] Try telling a friend that their behavior reveals a hidden feeling or thought, and chances are good they'll balk at the suggestion. They'll tell you you're wrong: How could they have a feeling they don't know about?

But still, the idea lives on. Nearly everyone in American society has heard about the unconscious. It even shows up in crossword puzzles. On some level it is affirmed day in and day out—whether by a white person crossing the street as a Black person approaches, an awkward truth revealed in a slip of the tongue, or by a sentiment stirred up by a memory long forgotten. We still keep the beast behind the cellar door, and we still don't realize we are doing so. The day I realized that the strange and rambling house embodied my unconscious mind, the dream vanished from my sleeping life, never to return.

Given the potential for ideas to shape our lives so profoundly, why wouldn't we want to help more children learn how to think about them, and create their own? And what would it take to do just that?

5

The Idea Workshop

In my entire life as a student, I remember only twice being given the opportunity to come up with my own ideas, a fact I consider typical and terrible.

—Eleanor Duckworth

Alice Hope felt sure she was on the path to be an artist. Willowy, with a wide, beautiful face and thin limbs, she wore narrow corduroys slung low on her hips and old-fashioned button-up shirts, not tucked in. She looked scruffy yet somehow chic. While at Reed College, she had met her future husband, and soon after graduating they had a baby girl. During her daughter's first years, Alice did make some paintings and sculptures, but she wasn't all in. Not then. She was uncertain of her artistic potential and absorbed by domestic life.

When her daughter was five, Alice took a teaching job in a small suburban school. She was given her own classroom of children ages six through ten, fifteen of them. She was told that she had carte blanche—that she should simply come up with ways to get the kids thinking hard, writing, making things, counting, and reading. I was advising the school at the time, and told her it would be great if she and the kids could work on a big project, something that others might eventually see or use. She didn't say anything when I told her that. I couldn't even tell if she heard me or not.

Alice comes across as thoughtful and slightly vague. She often pauses at unexpected places in her sentences when she speaks—not as if she needs time to form her thoughts or is nervous. More as if she isn't quite sure she wants to let the thought out. She has a way of talking about things that can bring the most pedestrian details a little out of focus. Once, during a faculty meeting about logistics, she was asked whether she wanted her class to have recess right after lunch. She didn't say yes or no. Instead, she paused several beats, looking at the woman who had posed the question as if she was both there and not there. "They often seem to do their best work after they've had some time to get a feel for the materials," she said finally. "I want them to know what it feels like to work on something even when nothing meaningful is happening." Another pause. "I think recess would be good. Then maybe we can spend the rest of the day working on something a little more visceral, less contemplative." It can take even the most determined and engaged person a little while to know just what she is talking about. In a room of conventionally trained elementary school teachers, she'd stand out—a single smudge of sage green amidst a sea of neat circles of primary blue.

The first few weeks of that year, other teachers passing by her room were often slightly confused by what they saw. Things seemed a little different from their own classrooms. While visiting the school, I watched two kids rush up to Alice, their faces flushed and angry, their voices strident, as they complained that another pair of children had invaded their designated work space, leaving paper and mess where they had been building their project, pushing them out of "their" area. Alice looked down at their hectic expressions with an inscrutable expression on her face. It almost seemed as if she had no idea what to say, or how to settle things down. Another, more experienced teacher might have promptly sent them back to their table to work it out with the other children. Or marched over to move the invaders to a different location. But Alice hesitated, then said in a quiet, almost distant voice, "This work is absorbing, isn't it? It's hard to make a story board. Do you want to lay your pages out on the long table over there?" The kids seemed rattled that she didn't firmly chastise the invaders, or tell them to quiet down. They stood there saying nothing for a moment, confused by her oblique response. Then they looked over at the long table she had pointed to. One of them shrugged slightly, then they took their work and spread it out in the new spot, refocused on the work itself.

Some kids didn't get her at first, but within a few weeks everyone seemed to have settled into the ways of her classroom. The children began to understand Alice's pace and her manner of communicating. Meanwhile, they did many of the activities that other children in the school were doing. They chose books to read, and wrote about what they were reading. They worked on numerical computation and basic geometry. They solved word problems and had morning meetings. They went to gym and they studied Egypt. Her rapport with children seemed unusual, but her curriculum did not seem particularly different from the others in her school.

Straws and Can Tabs

Then, in November, Alice told her students that they were going to start connecting straws. She brought in over forty boxes of plastic straws. She showed the group how you could pinch the end of one to connect it to another. She told them that each day they'd spend time putting straws together. "I think we should try to get into the

Guinness Book of World Records, for the longest straw chain." She left a few copies of the Guinness book lying around, so the children could see what it was. But she didn't say much more than that. In classic Alice fashion, she didn't mention that her real idea was for the students to "physically fathom the depth of the Mariana Trench—36,201 feet." Winning the record would be fun, but the enduring benefit would be coming to grips with vast quantities. She told me this as if to ask: Doesn't every teacher have a near goal and a far one?

Each day, she asked her students to connect some straws. At first, the other teachers and the parents were amused. It seemed like an okay craft, likely to calm the children and keep them busy when they had run out of steam for math or reading. Some murmured about the oddity of directing young children toward winning a place in a book of record feats. And why this one? So quirky. By March, a few of the kids were grumbling. They were tired of attaching straws. How long would they have to do this? Meanwhile, another group of kids, the ones who seemed to love sitting there fitting one straw to another, started chatting about the chain's length. Eventually, when they had finished putting all the segments together, how long would it be? What was the longest thing any of them had ever seen in real life? Was it possible to make a straw chain that would ring around the whole world? What would happen if you stood the whole thing upright? This last question segued into a twenty-five-minute digression about how the chain might be fortified since it would never stand straight up on its own.

The work was mundane. Their ruminations were anything but. By May, they had constructed a straw chain that measured just over 3.8 miles. Though they didn't reach the trench depth, they did break the record that year for longest straw chain, and won their mention in the *Guinness Book of World Records.*

After another year in the school, Alice left to move back to the city. Now and then, she did some part-time teaching in a neighborhood school because she missed working with children. But she spent most of her time making large sculptures from a variety of salvaged materials. Some years later, the school where she had launched the straw project asked her to fill in for another teacher's maternity leave. This time she'd be working with kids between the ages of eleven and fourteen. She said she would do it, if they were comfortable letting her class spend a great deal of time collecting, counting, and reusing can tabs. The class began the project in February, and toward the end of May the students had made an enormous sculpture of can tabs.

By then, Alice's focus had shifted almost completely from teacher to artist. At the end of that year, when her daughter began college, she returned full-time to working in her studio. She made very large sculptures, some of which were mounted on a wall, some of which sat on the floor. Almost all were at least five feet tall, and often just as wide. They were made of small pieces of metal and plastic—the can tab was a favorite medium. Many of them had the quality of chain mail from the middle ages. Their shapes were abstract and undulating. They resembled shields and waves, and some even looked like metal skins taken from large, imaginary animals. She also used the can tabs to make small things, like beautiful pieces of jewelry. Within five years she had begun selling her sculptures, showing in galleries, and winning commissions for large-scale works. But she missed making things with children. So, she suggested to the school where she had worked years before that she might come once a week, as an artist-in-residence, to build something with a group of students. The school was happy to have her.

I hadn't talked to her in years when she called me. "I know what I want to do with the kids where I'll be working," she said. "I want to hear what you think." We sat down over lemonade and she began to speak. She paused, as she so often does, looked past me, and then said, "I want to see if we can embody the unfathomable. I think I want to use can tabs to represent populations over time. I've been thinking about the subjectivity of size—for instance, the horizon. Do the kids realize that the horizon only looks like *something* because they are looking at it *from* a particular vantage point? I'm not interested in whether they can draw the horizon, or even what it looks like to them. I want them to think about subjectivity."

She continued: "Teachers are ingrained with the idea that children need to have 'real' or 'hands-on' experiences. Everyone insists that they can only learn abstract things like algebra if they can use concrete objects. Maybe so, but that doesn't mean abstract ideas are meaningless to them, does it? I think they like thinking about abstract ideas."

Alice was right. The single most important thing children can get out of their education is the inclination and facility to build their own ideas, and to explore and consider the ones other people put forth. Yet a deliberate focus on ideas is singularly absent from most classrooms. It's also completely missing from educational policy. Children are encouraged by teachers to master or practice any number of topics and skills. Policies are implemented to insure that children who don't know certain facts, or can't demonstrate key academic skills, are not promoted to the next grade. But the ability to pursue ideas is left to chance, often assumed to be the inevitable consequence of learning algebra and spelling, how to summarize a text, how to stand in a line, how to follow instructions, and all the other things we put energy into teaching. That assumption is wrong. The ability to pursue ideas is anything but inevitable. We're teaching everything but the most important thing.

If you ask a parent or teacher whether they value children's ideas, most will give you a surprised glance, as if you've asked them whether we should be kind to children. Most adults *think* that they think that children have ideas. But they don't *act* that way. Teachers, parents, and admiring onlookers may note the charm of a child's phrasing, laugh at their unusual choice of words, or admire their precocity when it seems that one of them understands a sophisticated notion. Relatives are ready to be amused by young children's unusual perceptions and impressed by a particular child's keen insights.

It has even become something of the fashion to consult children about their wishes and feelings about all manner of things. Eavesdrop in any park, restaurant, or classroom morning meeting and you will hear adults soliciting children's views. *Did it make you sad when your dog died? That story about ghosts scared you, didn't it?* Adults also often make a point of asking children for their preferences. *Did you enjoy the movie? What do you want to do this afternoon?* To be sure, there is value in paying attention to feelings and giving children a say in what happens. But this is not the same as taking their thoughts seriously, or helping them become better at building an idea.

Streetlights and Lightbulbs

When I was three, I attended a small preschool housed in the basement of a church. Most days, I got there riding in a child-seat on the front of my mother's bicycle. It was a short ride—maybe ten minutes, but the route took us through six traffic lights. My earliest childhood memory is a game my mother and I played as she pedaled along toward my school. She'd call out the color of the first light (say, "green light"), and then it was my turn to answer with a different color (perhaps, "yellow light"). Then she'd take another turn, and then back to me. Obviously, after three turns, we'd run out of the conventional colors of the signals—the game was to keep coming up with new colors that neither of us had already said. I remember it as a real brainteaser—which is why, I suppose, I still so vividly recall my best-ever turn. I triumphantly called out from my little perch, "Beige light!" Who would have dreamed up such a color? And for a traffic light, no less. "Beige light!" my mother exclaimed. "What a good idea!"

In retrospect, that may have been my first awareness that coming up with something in my head constituted an idea—a specific thought that might seem obvious or clever, unusual or mundane, but was, nevertheless, a thought of my own. Of course, I didn't possess words like *clever* and *mundane* to describe the qualities an idea might have. But I had a glimmer of what it felt like to think of something new or different. I got a rush I when I hit upon "beige light."

Most three-year-olds have similar lightbulb moments. But those fleeting thoughts are only the beginning. Over the next three years or so, they will acquire a panoply of skills that allow them to inquire, invent, and think about ideas.

Just to recap: children exhibit the rudiments of curiosity from the moment they are born. By three they can deliberately pursue whatever piques their interest, ask questions, and do deep dives into topics that really grab them. During the same period of time, their skills as inventors unfold, albeit along a more crooked path. From the moment they begin pretending and making up stories, in their second year, they are laying the groundwork for dreaming up new solutions to a wide array of problems. During that same period of development, they also begin to pursue more abstract ideas—chewing away at problems like mortality, identity, and simultaneity.

During the first five years of life, the psychological processes involved in inquiry, invention, and ideas play out somewhat independently of one another. Each follows a sequence of particular steps (the order of these steps is important, but the age at which a child reaches specific milestones is not). Somewhere around the fifth year of life, those strands converge, catapulting children into a new intellectual universe. By six, most children are capable of knowing what an idea is, and they understand what it means to have one.

At this point they can treat an idea as a mental object, something to weigh, critique, revise, or apply. They are able to apply their powers of inquiry and invention to intellectual problems that interest them. And yet, although nearly all children *can* pursue ideas, that doesn't mean they *do*. Whether a child gets better and better at considering ideas, or coming up with new ones, depends on the adults around them. Parents matter, and so do teachers.

The report cards and narrative forms used by most elementary schools contain certain standard headings: *understands number problems, adds and subtracts, checks work, uses evidence in reading comprehension, follows writing rubrics, follows instructions.* But it would be unfair and misleading to say that educators look at only these narrowly construed academic accomplishments. They do consider other characteristics, as well.

In the past fifteen years or so, for example, schools have also more explicitly taken on the responsibility to help children learn to get along, share, help one another, and be kind. Often this is talked about as character education, or social and emotional learning. Such features are typically clustered together, and referred to as the "soft skills," to mark a contrast between them and "hard" academic skills like math and reading. Sometimes the soft skills are hitched to another set of behaviors that have recently become popular to work on: self-control, focus, and the ability to follow directions, also known as executive functioning. A wave of important recent research has shown that children who can't tune out distractions, stick with a task, or delay receiving a reward are more likely to struggle in school. And the scientific studies are backed up by everyday experience. Teachers all across the country will tell you that more and more students seem out of control. Many teachers feel there is barely any time to focus on academics, because they use up so much keeping children from falling apart, in one way or another. And at least some of the research supports the idea that these abilities can be taught in school.

In sum, the educational system focuses enormous resources and attention on helping children acquire specific academic skills, learn fundamental information, and manage their own behavior. Yet you will rarely, if ever, come across a schoolwide curriculum or list of educational goals that emphasizes idea-building. Imagine assessing students' progress under some new headings: *poses interesting questions, speculates, sticks with a complex question and finds answers, articulates important problems and spends time solving them, can approach an idea from several perspectives, knows when an idea needs revision and knows how to do so.*

A skeptic might argue that getting better at having ideas doesn't require any specific deliberate educational attention—that children will have them whether we support the process or not. That would seem to be the prevalent assumption in our society. The evidence suggests otherwise. Even by the age of four, there are significant differences in how often children participate in conversations about abstract concepts, in their abilities to offer causal explanations for mysterious phenomena, and in their opportunities, as invited by adults, to discuss topics that go beyond the immediate or practical.[1] And those differences in children's very early experience with ideas are closely linked to various academic outcomes later on.[2] The children who turn out to learn most easily at school are the ones who, at a young age, heard more words, had more conversations, and talked more about the nonpractical. The children who score higher on aptitude tests in high school are the ones who read more books and developed bigger vocabularies.[3] At the very least, we now know that there are sturdy links between the intellectual experiences of early childhood and the academic successes of teenagers.

But it goes further than that. Collectively, the studies referenced above show that when children participate in the symbolized world—the world of words and numbers that articulate ideas—at an early age, they become more interested in and able to navigate that world as they get older. Recent evidence shows that young children can learn that different kinds of phenomena call for different kinds of explanations. Exposure, at a young age, to causal explanations has a profound impact on children's capacity to think well. In other words, if you want a person to readily inhabit the world of ideas when they are big, you should invite them into it when they are little.[4]

What does it look like when adults and children make it a more deliberate habit to think about ideas? It begins when adults explicitly highlight the ideas that crop up informally throughout a child's day. The four-year-old daughter of a friend of mine asked, "Daddy, what happens when you die?" You might recall from Chapter Four that adults tend to respond to such a question with answers like *You go to heaven* or *Everything stops* or *Don't worry—that won't happen for a long time.* But my friend gave a different kind of answer altogether: "A lot of people have different ideas about that."

With this brief and low-key response, he did something that more parents should do more often: he directed his daughter's attention to the fact that she was probing an idea. Instead of providing a partic-ular fact about death, he highlighted that people construct their un-derstanding of death. His response cracked open a door for his daughter to peek into the world of ideas. Such casual yet well-framed remarks often lead to more extended exchanges, in which children pursue their thoughts out loud, trying out the techniques and strate-gies required to consider an idea fully.

Liz Bonawitz, a developmental psychologist, describes an exchange between a four-year-old-girl and her six-year-old brother on their way to school one morning with their mother. They have been talking about leprechauns.

She: They make a big mess—like pee green in the toilet.

He: I don't think they exist.

She: Oh yeah—then how does the toilet get green?

He: I think adults put paint in the toilet.

She: That doesn't make sense—why would adults try to make a mess?

He: I don't know, but I don't think leprechauns exist. I mean, I used to believe in them like you, but now I don't think so.

Mother: What made you change your mind?

He: Well, two things. First, because I think it's suspicious that no one has ever caught one. Second, because I have only ever read about them in fiction books. If they aren't in nonfiction books, then they are probably not real.[5]

What stands out in this casual conversation, which simply popped up on the way to school, is that at one point or another, all three participants comment on how they know what they know. The brother talks about sources of information, the importance of firsthand evidence, and how one's beliefs can change. The mother asks what made his beliefs change. And even the four-year-old voices a rejection of a claim because it "doesn't make sense." Everyone is actively considering an idea (the existence of leprechauns), and they are doing it out loud, together. Treating a child as someone interested in ideas and able to discuss them has a significant impact on that child's intellectual future.

The elements of having ideas come naturally to young children. But those elements converge and lead to a more powerful, skilled pursuit of ideas only when adults provide certain kinds of support. Here is a set of things adults can do, day in and day out, to help children learn to build ideas.

Highlight ideas. Notice when a child seems to be working on an idea. The language of speculations, schemes, and hypotheses provides children with a powerful tool for their own intellectual forays, and lets them know that building an idea is a valuable endeavor. Talk about where ideas come from, how one changes over time, how people decide whether an idea is a good one or not, and what effect ideas have had on you. When I jauntily proposed "beige light," my mother could have responded in any number of ways. She could've ignored it. She could have said, "Beige can't be the color of a light." She also could have said only "Terrific!" or "Good one!" She could have been simply enthusiastic. But instead, what she said opened up a whole new world to me. She said, "What a good idea."

Notice the processes children use when they invent. Ask them whether they knew ahead of time what they wanted to make. Ask them what problem they were trying to solve. Notice how many iterations their invention required. Making the process explicit will not ruin things. That said, this needn't turn into another lesson, and not every invention requires commentary. Also, periodically point out the connections between making *things* and making *ideas*. Children need to acquire a framework for thinking about their own thoughts. And they can only do that if they are regularly encouraged to talk about the processes they use for fabricating things and ideas.

Spend time every day identifying the hypotheses and speculations embedded in casual talk. Be more than ready to talk about it when your own speculation about something turns out to be wrong. Encourage children to think about how they will know whether their speculation is right or not. What evidence will prove them right or wrong? It's more than okay for someone to think through an idea they hate or feel sure they will eventually discard. Before telling children they are right or wrong, or have touched on a dangerous topic, ask them to say more about what they have in mind. Make it a habit to explore people's reasons for thinking what they think.

Evelyn, a first-grade teacher I've known for many years, sent me a text one day out of the blue. One of her students, Isaiah, had burst out in morning meeting with a new revelation: "Dumb people don't live as long as smart people." The other children looked at him impassively. Evelyn couldn't tell, in that quick instant, what they thought of his proposal—maybe they were wondering which of them was dumb. Evelyn was thrown. His statement sounded nutty.

"What? What do mean, Isaiah?" So far, so good. She had invited him to expand on his cryptic comment.

"My cat was dumb," he explained, "and she crossed the road without looking, and got hit by a car and died."

Evelyn thought his answer ludicrous—that it revealed faulty logic. When she shared it with me, it was with sarcasm: "I might have to explain Darwin's theory to him." Now it was my turn to be thrown, and I asked her what she meant. "He obviously doesn't know that people don't live longer because they're *smart*—it's whether they were born in good health, and stuff like that."

But she was the one who really needed correcting. Isaiah was on the edge of making an interesting speculation: perhaps higher IQ is favored in unpredictable environments. There's a good chance that if Evelyn had encouraged him to develop his idea, rather than dismissing it as wacky, they might both have advanced their understanding of evolution. It was one of those fleeting moments that offer adults golden opportunities to help children develop their fledgling ideas. She let the comment drop because she worried it might be hurtful somehow to other children and believed it was misguided. She could have instead helped him arrive at the hypothesis buried within his comment. She could have suggested they identify the assumptions implicit in his comment, and explore them further. She might have invited the other children to help think of some evidence that would test his hypothesis. Children are inclined toward intellectual work. But they need guidance to get better at it, and many opportunities to engage in it.

The renowned education scholar Deborah Ball was an elementary school teacher when she was young. In a revelatory film clip of her classroom work, we see her talking to her fourth-grade class. A title running across the bottom of the screen explains that she has just been teaching her students about odd and even numbers. But when the clip begins, she is talking about something else. She has just asked them to comment on an all-school meeting they had attended the day before. One little boy raises his hand and says, "I don't have anything about the meeting yesterday, but I was just thinking about six—'cause I was just thinking, it could be an odd number too . . ." He looks slightly stressed, and absorbed by his inner thoughts, but he continues to elaborate. Ball, a master teacher, draws him out, getting him to explain fully to the class that he thinks the number six can be both odd and even because it contains two sets of three, and three itself is an odd number. Ball could correct him. But she doesn't. Instead, she invites others to respond. What ensues is remarkable.

The children spend more than seven full minutes collectively mulling over his suggestion. A few children speculate on the reasoning that might have led their classmate to conclude that six is an odd and an even number. A few children get up and show, with varying degrees of mathematical sophistication, why it's just not possible. One little girl gets up, grabs the wooden pointer, and walks over to the blackboard on which there is a number line. Beginning with the numeral two she taps every other number on the number line and points out that this includes six, thereby excluding it from the class of "odd numbers."

Finally, a delicate looking girl with long black hair, not nearly as tall as the others in the group, raises her hand high and says, "I think I know why he said that." She notes that six is made up of three groups of two, and that he might think the fact that it contained three groups—and three is an odd number—qualified it, too, as an odd number. The girl then continues, "but that's wrong. It can't be even *and* odd." In the video you can see her getting increasingly energized, worked up even, as she tries to articulate what's bubbling around in her mind. She asks permission to go to the chalkboard, where she joins the boy, who is slouching against the chalk tray, having just used the board to explain his thinking to the skeptics in the group. He looks interested, and less and less certain of his thinking as the others chime in.

After taking a moment to gather her thoughts, the little girl says, "Mmm, let me think. I mean, if you say that six could be an odd number why don't you say other numbers could be odd?" She hesitates, clearly trying to come up with another example that would also contain an odd number of groups. Within eight seconds she has hit upon an example. "Take ten," she says. She draws ten circles in a row, on the board. You could say that it has five groups of two. Why don't you say ten is an odd number for the same reason? If you say that, then pretty soon all the even numbers would be odd, and then there would be no—no difference between even and odd, and then we wouldn't even be having this discussion!" She ends her argument in a triumphant yet slightly agitated tone.[6]

Though some of the children appear much more involved than others, all of them are listening and interested. Any classroom teacher will tell you that seven straight minutes of focused conversation on the status of a number, by a group of nine-year-old children, is extraordinary. Ball's classroom didn't just happen to have this extended, serious, probing exchange about the nature of numbers. She worked hard, probably for months, to get the children to take their own and other people's ideas seriously. She gave them problems that invited attention. She knew enough about the subject of numbers to highlight their most interesting or problematic thoughts, and to be comfortable nudging them toward greater clarity, logic, and exegesis. She created a culture of ideas. All within a diverse class of nine-year-old children in a Midwestern public school.

Make it a habit with the children you know to ask the following questions: What would make this true? What if I'm wrong? What might happen if . . . ? Invite them to join you as you mull things over out loud and entertain uncertainty, saying "I have to think more about that," or deciding, as the journalist Ezra Klein often puts it, to consider "a perspective not my own."

Encourage children to build ideas with other people. Instill the practice of pushing back. In the magnificent children's book *Lion*, William Pène du Bois tells a story of 114 artists who work in a huge studio up in the clouds, designing animals for Earth. One day, the artist in charge, named Foreman, decides he's going to invent a new animal. He has already decided what to name the creature; it will be called "Lion." After his first rendering, he takes his drawing to one of the other artists working at a drafting table.

"Tell me, in one word," he says, "what is wrong with the Lion."

The other artist looks at the creature Foreman has drawn, and responds: "Size."

Foreman realizes his lion is far too small for the magnificent creature he has in mind. He goes back to his own drawing table, and makes it much bigger. Then he shows his picture to another artist: "Tell me in one word, what is wrong with the Lion."

The artist says, "Feathers."

Foreman realizes a creature cannot have feathers *and* fur, so he blends the feathers until they look like a huge fluffy mane. With more feedback from more artists, the Lion also sees his many bright colors changed to a silky brown coat, and his tiny legs made longer and stronger. Finally, the sound he makes transforms from a "peep peep" to a "ROAR." It's a gorgeous book, but also a wonderful parable about the value of getting input from others to improve on an idea.[7]

City Neighbors School is a network of public schools that lies in one of the poorest districts of Baltimore. On your way to the schools themselves, you have to pass through desolate city blocks of dilapidated buildings and vacant lots. When I visited, the streets around the school looked appallingly neglected—empty and unfriendly. But once I walked into the elementary and high school buildings, a different world enveloped me. Adults and teachers were talking, working, and hanging out. The sense of a multi-aged learning community was palpable. In almost every classroom I visited, from the kindergarten to the third grade, and in the high school, there were visible signs that groups of people were pursuing very interesting questions—questions that obviously felt pressing to children and were not easily answerable.

In a third-grade classroom, the students were keeping two lists: one of things that were alive, and the other of things that were not. On a separate large sheet of paper, they were identifying the methods by which they decided what was alive and what was not. Even in the short time of my visit, I overheard several small groups of students discussing what constitutes "being alive." The older children at the school took such contemplation one step further.

In an eighth-grade class, the students were trying, both individually and as a group, to come to some agreement on a question: Is conflict good? They spent more than three months exploring various answers, and fleshing out the reasons for their answers. Finding facts to inform and support the answers was an essential part of their work. They argued with one another. Some changed their minds.

Finally, in a ninth-grade class, students and teachers were spending a term on another question: Is life in America getting better? It's easy to imagine how a diverse group of teenagers might really sink their teeth into such a question. It's equally easy to imagine how a teacher could use such a provocative and relevant question as a springboard for stretching the students' intellectual muscles.

Let children construct their own problems. Students are asked to solve problems all day long. But most of the time, an adult (the teacher or textbook author) poses the problems. It is assumed that children's eagerness to "get it right" will motivate them to think well. And some of the time that's true. But in fact, a close look at how innovation develops suggests that children's thinking is better when they figure out what the problem is themselves, and when they truly care about it—when it feels like a problem to them.

Catherine Snow wanted to find out how middle-school students might learn to be better writers and engage in more academic exchanges. She argued that such exchanges demand five things: perspective-taking, providing warrants for one's views, anticipating counterargument, holding what she calls an epistemic orientation, and using an authoritative or writerly voice to convey those views. Snow and her colleagues assigned some sixth-grade classes to study a variety of interesting topics in preparation for writing short essays. But they asked a separate set of sixth-grade classrooms instead to prepare to debate one another on topics that were on the students' minds: whether junk food should be allowed in the cafeteria, the length of the school day, and whether there should be mandatory national service. The students in the latter set felt strongly about the topics, threw themselves into the academic challenges of the work, and were eager to win their debates. In the process, their vocabularies expanded, their writing skills improved, and their powers of argument soared past the children who were taught in the more conventional way.[8]

At sixteen, Greta Thunberg had already skipped school more than thirty times, preferring to stand in the center of Stockholm with a poster demanding that her government act to prevent climate change. Several years earlier, she might not have seemed very exceptional. She did well in school, she struggled with depression, she watched television. A profile in the *New York Times* suggests, however, that she was especially thoughtful:

> Like many children, she watched educational films about the melting Arctic and the fate of the polar bears and the marine mammals bloated with plastic. But unlike other children, she couldn't let them go. "I became very affected. I began thinking about it all the time and I became very sad," she said. "Those pictures were stuck in my head."

Also unlike many other children, she grew into a highly visible and effective activist. What began as a solitary gesture of defiance soon garnered attention in many countries. When UK prime minister Theresa May criticized British schoolchildren following suit with similar protests—saying that the children were wasting valuable "lesson time"—Thunberg responded in a tweet. "But then again, political leaders have wasted 30 yrs of inaction. And that is slightly worse." In the *Times* profile, she comments that activism helped her overcome depression: "I'm happier now. . . . I have meaning. I have something I have to do."[9]

For students to pursue ideas, and more importantly, to become better at it—that is, to learn to base their ideas on evidence, revise them in smart ways, consider an idea's weaknesses, think about its limitations, imagine its applications and implications, and connect it to other ideas—they need chances to work on ideas that matter. For children to get anything meaningful out of solving a problem, the problem must be a problem to *them*. Make sure that at least some of the time, children are given a chance to explain phenomena that are mysterious to them, and solve problems that they feel a burning need to solve.

Greta's ambitions are unusually high, of course. Most of the time, children try to solve more immediate and less consequential problems. When my nephew Charlie was about eight, I took him to the beach. As I stretched out my towel to lie in the sun, Charlie began scanning the shoreline. Within sixty seconds he had noticed something and made a dash for it. About two hundred feet from us lay a huge log—maybe five feet long and a foot in diameter. I watched out of the corner of my eye as Charlie began rolling the log closer to where we had settled. He finally got it where he wanted it. Then he began to dig. He dug and dug, for nearly forty minutes. Then he called his younger brother over to help him push the base to the edge of the hole, where they proceeded with great effort to hoist the log upright in the hole. Then they began the hard work of filling in around the base, so that the log stood up securely. Finally, nearly an hour after he had begun, Charlie's goal became clear. He and his brother took turns clamoring to the top using one another's interlaced hands as a stepstool. Once on top, each of them would take a flying leap off, landing in the soft wet sand that swirled around their jungle gym. They played at this for the rest of the afternoon. At some point, Charlie grabbed my hand and dragged me over to see what he had made. He was slightly winded from the building and the jumping, but triumphant: "See what I did? See what I did? I saw the log, I had an idea, and I put it into action!"

Children need to have a sense of purpose or use for their solutions and their explorations.

Give ideas plenty of time. My interest in examining how children learn to build ideas was sparked by the observation that children regularly ask series of questions in pursuit of a larger theme. These questions typically unfold over a significant period of time. If I had only captured isolated moments in a child's life, I could not have noticed the themes. Similarly, children's inventions are often iterative; a new kind of fort, or a new story, does not emerge in one play session. Sometimes a child will tell twenty stories on a topic, changing and revising their basic narrative as they retell the tale. The same is true of the physical structures they build—traps, habitats, and robots. Actually, in this regard, young children are not too different from adults whose inventions have affected the lives of many. The seeds of most good ideas usually rest on a wide variety of previous experiences and a fair amount of expertise. Moreover, a seed of an idea is just a beginning. Most important inventions are the end result of a long process of revision, trial and error, and correction. Children need time to develop their ideas.

The school that hired Alice insisted she could work with the children only one day a week. Then they said she could only work with the students after classes had ended, on Friday afternoons, when the full-time faculty held their weekly meetings. The faculty sent the students to her in large groups, each for an hour. The other teachers felt that all the children should give it a go, and that sending them in smaller groups would be inefficient. These constraints worried her. It seemed as if the project was being treated like an afterthought—an activity for when the students had run out of steam for their "regular work." She was worried. I was just exasperated. I have seen this happen in schools again and again. The less important tasks take up a lot of time, and the more important work gets shunted to the periphery.

Nevertheless, Alice arrived that first Friday with a huge heap of can tabs. The children walked into the room with wary, interested looks on their faces. "Hi, my name is Alice," she began. "I'm an artist. I'm going to be coming every Friday over the year, to work on one project, and we'll use these can tabs. The project will help us see millions, miles, time itself—we're going to make a continuous line."

That first day, Alice struggled with the children. They threw the can tabs, whipped the chains that had already been put together, and chatted noisily. A few lay in the pile of can tabs, one even stepped through it, and they didn't listen. Alice called me, frustrated. She felt that the size of the group got in the way of any real conversation about the tabs and what they were making, and most importantly, about what they were thinking. Many of the kids, she reported, seemed determined to "win" by connecting the most can tabs. Others were fixated on finding the "special" tabs—whatever those were. She thought they craved variation. But a few, she noticed, were different. They didn't seem to care that they were beating the others, though they did end up making the longest chains. They seemed more engrossed in the action they were performing than the other kids did.

Alice recorded the questions children asked as they worked and we reviewed them later. We noticed they kept coming back to four themes: How were they going to attach all the chains into one? Would they run out of material? Why had she chosen can tabs? And what might infinity look like? But still, it wasn't playing out the way she had expected. She was unsure that it would turn into something mean-ingful for the children. "I don't know if this is going to work," she admitted. I couldn't tell if she was worried they wouldn't build some-thing beautiful, or afraid they wouldn't get anything out of it. But she kept going, and the kids kept coming back on Fridays. Each week a few more found their way into the endeavor. The strong core group kept adding fellow builders. The conversations continued. By April, Alice knew the can tab project should be called Aeon.

The last time we discussed the project, Alice said, "I think some time in the early spring, they began to get it. And they've gotten so good. I told them, a while back, 'We're only here for an hour, and every one of you can string a year in an hour. This is what a year looks like.'" She held up a chain on which 365 tabs had been strung—a necklace thick with metal disks, its edges waving in and out unevenly—heavy and beautiful. "Sometimes they string for more than an hour just to make another year," Alice said. "Sometimes they argue about whether they've strung six months, or two years. Once in a while, nine months just falls off—they've learned so much about gravity. They're flinging it around and some drops off, and then all they have is twenty-eight days. Then they have to begin stringing more. They really love wearing a year around their necks."

In late May, a local gallery showed all seven pieces comprising Aeon. One looked like a giant Slinky, inching and stretching its way across the entire gallery floor. Another looked like a huge, specialized, industrial pipe. It began on the floor and rose all the way to the ceiling, more than a foot in diameter. Neon-yellow and red labels hung from some of its rings, indicating the ages of people represented by various lengths of the tabs. Another looked like a colossal garland looped across the floor, and climbing up and over the sides of several wooden pillars, finally reaching all the way out of one of the gallery windows.

The sculptures involved many children working for many hours over the course of eight months. They put together structures that transformed time into objects you could touch, walk around, and look at. The work itself was powerful, bold, and complex. It was magnificent. Less easy to see but even more arresting were the ideas that doing the work had evoked in the children. During the eight months they talked about the nature of time and space, the challenge of embodying an idea in three dimensions, the relationship between different metrics (can tabs and years, for instance), and what it was like to contemplate infinity. Sometimes their discussions were sustained and coherent. Other times, their thoughts came across as a collection of comments and moments whose significance might be lost on anyone but a focused observer. None of their ruminations could have happened if the project had been confined to a few weeks—or if it hadn't been guided by an adult with a ferocious interest not only in children, but also in the ideas themselves. Imagine what might have happened if Alice had been able to work with the children several days a week, in smaller groups, during the school day. Good ideas take time.

We now know that young children are avid thinkers. They are ready to detect the mysteries of life, and eager to solve them. But that is only a starting point. Whether they grow up to a life of inquiry, invention, and ideas—or a life without these—depends on nothing more, or less, than the company of adults who stoke their intellectual fires.

Notes
Acknowledgments
Index

Notes

1. Prelude

1. J. Seabrook, "The Flash of Genius," *New Yorker,* January 11, 1993.

2. L. Peake, "The Great Pacific Cleanup," Resource 78 (Autumn 2014). Also see C. Kormann, "A Grand Plan to Clean the Great Pacific Garbage Patch," *New Yorker,* February 4, 2019; and B. Slat, "How the Oceans Can Clean Themselves," TEDx Delft, October 5, 2012, https://www.tedxdelft.nl /2012/08/performer-boyan-how-the-oceans-can-clean-themselves/.

3. R. Dawkins, *The Selfish Gene* (Oxford, UK: Oxford University Press, 1976).

4. D. Kahneman, *Thinking Fast and Slow* (New York: Farrar, Straus and Giroux, 2011).

5. L. Festinger, H. Riecken, and S, Schachter, *When Prophecy Fails: A Social and Psychological Study of a Modern Group that Predicted the Destruction of the World* (New York: Harper & Row, 1964).

6. C. M. Steel and J. Aronson, "Stereotype Threat and the Intellectual Test Performance of African Americans," *Journal of Personality and Social Psychology* 69, no. 5 (1995): 797–811.

7. S. Metcalf, "Neoliberalism: The Idea that Swallowed the World," *Guardian,* August 18, 2017, https://www.theguardian.com/news/2017/aug/18 /neoliberalism-the-idea-that-changed-the-world.

8. For two examples of such work, see B. B. Henderson, "Parents and Exploration: The Effect of Context on Individual Differences," in *Exploratory Behavior. Children Development,* 55, no. 4 (1984): 1237–1245; and G. Lowenstein, "The Psychology of Curiosity: A Review and Reinterpretation, *Psychological Bulletin* 116, no. 1 (1994): 75–98.

2. Inquiry

Epigraph: Four-year-old child in CHILDES TalkBank database. Access the database at https://childes.talkbank.org/.

1. J. Kagan, *Surprise, Uncertainty, and Mental Structures* (Cambridge, MA: Harvard University Press, 2002).

2. K. Nelson. *Young Minds in Social Worlds: Experience, Meaning, and Memory* (Cambridge, MA: Harvard University Press, 2007).

3. K. Nelson, Event Knowledge: Structure and Function in Development (Hillsdale, NJ: Erlbaum, 1986); S. Engel, *The Hungry Mind: The Origins of Curiosity in Childhood* (Cambridge, MA: Harvard University Press, 2016).

4. G. S. Hall, *The Contents of Children's Minds on Entering School* (New York: E. L. Kellogg, 1893).

5. D. E. Berlyne, *Conflict, Arousal, and Curiosity* (New York: McGraw-Hill, 1960); D. E. Berlyne, "Curiosity and Exploration," *Science* 153, no. 3731 (1966): 25–33.

6. C. K. Hsee and B. Ruan, "The Pandora Effect: The Power and Peril of Curiosity," *Psychological Science* 27, no. 5 (2016): 659–666.

7. L. E. Schulz and E. B. Bonawitz, "Serious Fun: Preschoolers Engage in More Exploratory Play When Evidence Is Confounded," *Developmental Psychology* 43, no. 4 (2007): 1045–1050.

8. C. Cook, N. D. Goodman, and L. E. Schulz, "Where Science Starts: Spontaneous Experiments in Preschoolers' Exploratory Play," *Cognition* 120, no. 3 (2011): 341–349.

9. R. W. Magid, M. Sheskin, and L. E. Shulz, "Imagination and the Generation of New Ideas," *Cognitive Development* 34 (2015): 99–110.

10. D. Kelemen, M. A. Callanan, K. Casler, and D. R. Pérez-Granados, "Why Things Happen: Teleological Explanation in Parent-Child Conversations," *Developmental Psychology* 41, no. 1 (2005): 251–264.

11. S. M. Baker and J. W. Gentry, "Kids as Collectors: A Phenomenological Study of First and Fifth Graders," *Advances in Consumer Research* 23 (1996): 132–137.

12. M. M. Chouinard, P. L. Harris, and M. P. Maratsos, "Children's Questions: A Mechanism for Cognitive Development," *Monographs of the Society for Research in Child Development* 72, no. 1 (2007): i–129.

13. M. Gauvain, R. L. Munroe, and H. Beebe, "Children's Questions in Cross-Cultural Perspective: A Four-Culture Study," *Journal of Cross-Cultural Psychology* 44, no. 7 (2013): 1148–1165.

14. Gauvain, Munroe, and Beebe, "Children's Questions in Cross-Cultural Perspective," 1160, quoting B. MacWhinney and C. Snow, "The Child Language Data Exchange System," *Journal of Child Language* 12, no. 2 (1985): 271–295.

15. M. L. Rowe, K. A. Leech, and N. Cabrera, "Going beyond Input Quantity: *Wh*-Questions Matter for Toddlers' Language and Cognitive Development," *Cognitive Science* 41 (2017): 162–179.

16. P. L. Harris, *Trusting What You're Told: How Children Learn from Others* (Cambridge, MA: Harvard University Press, 2012). Also see P. L. Harris and M. A. Koenig. "Trust in Testimony: How Children Learn about Science and Religion," *Child Development* 77, no. 3 (2006): 505–524.

17. G. Wells, *The Meaning Makers: Children Learning Language and Using Language to Learn* (Portsmouth, NH: Heinemann Educational, 1986).

18. B. Hart and T. R. Risley, *Meaningful Differences in the Everyday Experience of Young American Children* (Baltimore, MD: Paul H. Brookes, 1995).

19. P. L. Harris, *Trusting what you're told: How children learn from others.* (Cambridge, MA: Harvard University Press, 2012). Also see P. L. Harris and M. A. Koenig. "Trust in Testimony: How Children Learn about Science and Religion," *Child Development* 77, no. 3 (2006): 505–524; and J. D. Lane and P. L. Harris, "Confronting, Representing, and Believing Counterintuitive Concepts: Navigating the Natural and the Supernatural," *Perspectives on Psychological Science* 9 no. 2 (2014): 144–160.

20. S. Carey, *The Origin of Concepts* (New York: Oxford University Press, 2009).

21. Chouinard, Harris, and Maratsos, *Children's Questions.*

22. T. H. Beery and K. S Lekies. "Childhood Collecting in Nature: Quality Experience in Important Places," in *Children's Geographies: Special Viewpoint Collection: Youth-full Geographies* 17, no. 1 (2019): 118–131.

23. Chouinard, Harris, and Maratsos, *Children's Questions,* 50, fig. 20.

24. Chouinard, Harris, and Maratsos, *Children's Questions.*

25. M. T. Chi, R. Glaser, and M. J. Farr, *The Nature of Expertise* (New York: Psychology Press, 2014).

26. J. Piaget, *The Child's Conception of the World,* trans. J. Tomlinson and A. Tomlinson (London: Kegan Paul, Trench, Trubner, 1929).

27. For an excellent set of papers describing first approaches to using computers to model the developing mind, see R. Siegler, ed., *Children's Thinking: What Develops?* (New York: Psychology Press, 1981).

28. M. T. Chi, J. E. Hutchinson, and A. F. Robin, "How Inferences about Novel Domain-Related Concepts Can Be Constrained by Structured Knowledge," *Merrill-Palmer Quarterly (1982–),* 27–62. For an example of the psychologists arguing at the time that expertise in a domain is related to a child's "level of development," see D. Klahr, "Information Processing Approaches to Cognitive Development," in R. Vasta, ed., *Annals of Child Development* (Greenwich, CT: JAI Press, 1989), 131–185. Republished in R. Vasta, R., ed., *Six Theories of Child Development* (London: Jessica Kingsley Publishers, 1992).

29. C. Gobbo and M. Chi, "How Knowledge Is Structured and Used by Expert and Novice Children," *Cognitive Development* 1, no. 3 (1986): 221–237.

30. Gobbo and Chi, "How Knowledge Is Structured," 225.

31. Gobbo and Chi, "How Knowledge Is Structured," 228.

32. A. L. Brown, "Transforming Schools into Communities of Thinking and Learning about Serious Matters," *American Psychologist* 52, no. 4 (1997): 399–413.

33. A. Newman, "William Reese, Leading Seller of Rare Books, Is Dead at 62," obituary, *New York Times,* June 15, 2018.

34. F. Spufford, *The Child That Books Built: A Life in Reading* (New York: Henry Holt / Metropolitan, 2002), quote page 81.

35. R. Mead, *My Life in Middlemarch* (New York: Broadway Books, 2014).

36. CHILDES TalkBank, https://childes.talkbank.org/; B. MacWhinney, *The CHILDES Project: Tools for Analyzing Talk, vol. 2: The Database,* 3rd ed. (New York: Psychology Press, 2014); B. MacWhinney and C. Snow, "The Child Language Data Exchange System," *Journal of Child Language* 12, no. 2 (1985): 271–295.

37. Research conducted with students was in the context of the Inquiry, Invention, and Ideas advanced psychology seminar at Williams College, 2018.

38. P. L. Harris, "Children's Understanding of Death: From Biology to Religion," *Philosophical Transactions of the Royal Society B: Biological Sciences* 373, no. 1754 (2018): 20170266.

39. Access the database at https://childes.talkbank.org/access/Eng-NA /Braunwald.html.

40. P. L. Harris, *The Work of the Imagination* (Oxford, UK: Blackwell, 2000), 168. Chouinard, Harris, and Maratsos, "Children's Questions," 5.

41. S. Isaacs, *Intellectual Growth in Young Children* (London: Routledge and Kegan Paul, 1931); S. Isaacs, *Social Development in Young Children* (London: Routledge, 1933).

42. Isaacs, *Social Development,* quotes on 190, 191, 193.

43. J. Colantonio and E. Bonawitz, "Awesome Play: Awe Increases Preschooler's Exploration and Discovery," OSF Preprints. May 16. doi:10.31219/ osf.io/pjhrq.

44. J. McPhetres, "Oh, The Things You Don't Know: Awe Promotes Awareness of Knowledge Gaps and Science Interest," *Cognition and Emotion* 33, no. 8 (2019): 1599–1615.

45. Chouinard, "Children's Questions"; P. L. Harris, *Trusting What You're Told: How Children Learn from Others* (Cambridge, MA: Harvard University Press, 2012); P. L. Harris, D. T. Bartz, and M. L. Rowe, "Young Children Communicate Their Ignorance and Ask Questions," *Proceedings of the National Academy of Sciences of the United States of America* 114, no. 30 (2017): 7884–7891; K. H. Corriveau and K. Kurkul, "Why Does Rain Fall?": Children Prefer to Learn from an Informant Who Uses Noncircular Explanations, *Child Development* 85 (2014): 1827–1835; K. E. Kurkul and K. H. Corriveau, "Question, Explanation, Follow-Up: A Mechanism for Learning from Others?" *Child Development* 89, no. 1 (2018): 280–294.

46. J. I. Rotgans and H. G. Schmidt, "The Relation between Individual Interest and Knowledge Acquisition," *British Educational Research Journal* 43, no. 2 (2017): 350–371.

3. Invention

Epigraph: B. Rose, "One of the Most Vital, Radical, and Optimistic Artists in the Past Century, Claes Oldenburg," *Interview* 45, no. 10 (Dec. 2015 / Jan 2016): 150–167, 154.

1. R. Bolton, "Place Prosperity vs. People Prosperity Revisited: An Old Issue with a New Angle," *Urban Studies* 29, no. 2 (1992): 185–203, quote on 194.

2. L. S. Vygotsky, *Thought and Language* (Cambridge, MA: MIT Press, 1962); S. Engel, *The Stories Children Tell: Making Sense of the Narratives of Childhood* (New York: W. H. Freeman, 1995).

3. M. Root-Bernstein, *Inventing Imaginary Worlds* (New York: Rowman and Littlefield, 2014).

4. S. R. Beck, I. A. Apperly, J. Chappell, C. Guthrie, and N. Cutting, "Making Tools Isn't Child's Play," *Cognition* 119, no. 2 (2011): 301–306.

5. N. Cutting, I. A. Apperly, and S. R. Beck, "Why Do Children Lack the Flexibility to Innovate Tools?" *Journal of Experimental Child Psychology* 109, no. 4 (2011): 497–511.

6. "Overlooked No More: Bette Nesmith Graham, Who Invented Liquid Paper," obituary, *New York Times,* July 11, 2018.

7. D. Faulkner, "Does a Lack of Knowledge Prevent Young Children From Inventing When They Otherwise Could?," Williams College Honors Thesis, 2019.

8. K. Neldner, J. Redshaw, S. Murphy, K. Tomaselli, J. Davis, B. Dixson, and M. Nielsen, "Creation across Culture: Children's Tool Innovation Is Influenced by Cultural and Developmental Factors," *Developmental Psychology* 55, no. 4 (2019): 877–889.

9. L. S. Vygotsky, *Thought and Language.*

10. A. Bell, R. Chetty, X. Jaravel, N. Petkova, and J. van Reenen, "Who Becomes an Inventor in America? The Importance of Exposure to Innovation," *Quarterly Journal of Economics* 134, no. 2 (2018): 647–713.

11. W. Sandford, "Does Language Help Children Invent?," Unpublished Honors Thesis, Williams College, 2020.

12. A similar finding was reported by Elizabeth Bonawitz and her colleagues. Children in their study engaged less in creative exploration of materials if they had been provided with instruction on a use of those things. E. Bonawitz, P. Shafto, H. Gweon, N. D. Goodman, E. Spelke, and L. Schulz, "The Double-Edged Sword of Pedagogy: Instruction Limits Spontaneous Exploration and Discovery," *Cognition* 120, no. 3 (2011): 322–330.

13. A. Meltzoff, "Understanding the Intentions of Others: Reenactments of Intended Acts by 18-Month-Old Children," *Developmental Psychology* 31, no. 5 (1995): 838–850.

14. A. N. Meltzoff and R. Brooks, "'Like Me' as a Building Block for Understanding Other Minds: Bodily Acts, Attention, and Intention," in B. F. Malle, L. J. Moses, and D. A. Baldwin (eds.), *Intentions and Intentionality: Foundations of Social Cognition* (Cambridge, MA: MIT Press, 2001): 171–191.

15. M. A. Defeyter and T. P. German, "Acquiring an Understanding of Design: Evidence from Children's Insight Problem Solving," *Cognition* 89, no. 2 (2003): 133–155. Also see K. Duncker and L. S. Lees, "On Problem-Solving," *Psychological Monographs* 58, no. 5 (1945), i.

16. The "Alternative Uses Test" was developed by Joy Paul Guilford in the 1960s to measure what he termed "spontaneous flexibility" and is now widely called divergent thinking. J. P. Guilford, "The Structure of Intellect," *Psychological Bulletin* 53, no. 4 (1956): 267–293.

17. A. Gopnik, S. O'Grady, C. G. Lucas, T. L. Griffiths, A. Wente, S. Bridgers, R. Aboody, H. Fung, and R. E. Dahl, "Changes in Cognitive Flexibility and Hypothesis Search across Human Life History from Childhood to Adolescence to Adulthood," *Proceedings of the National Academy of Sciences* 114, no. 30 (2017): 7892–7899.

18. A. Gopnik and D. M. Sobel, "Detecting Blickets: How Young Children Use Information about Novel Causal Powers in Categorization and Induction," *Child Development* 71, no. 5, 1205–1222. Also see David Dobbs, "Playing for All Kinds of Possibilities," *New York Times,* April 23, 2013.

19. C. G. Lucas, S. Bridgers, T. L. Griffiths, and A. Gopnik, "When Children Are Better (Or at Least More Open-Minded) Learners Than Adults: Developmental Differences in Learning the Forms of Causal Relationships," *Cognition* 131, no. 2 (2015): 284–299.

20. A. Gopnik, T. L. Griffiths, and C. G. Lucas, "When Younger Learners Can Be Better (Or At Least More Open-Minded) than Older Ones," *Current Directions in Psychological Science* 24, no. 2 (2015): 87–92.

21. Lucas et al., "When Children Are Better."

22. Beck et al. "Making Tools Isn't Child's Play"; Cutting et al., "Why Do Children Lack the Flexibility."

23. V. Horner and A. Whiten, "Causal Knowledge and Imitation / Emulation Switching in Chimpanzees (Pan troglodytes) and Children (Homo sapiens)," *Animal Cognition* 8, no. 3 (2005): 164–181.

24. K. Carr, R. L. Kendal, and E. G. Flynn, "Imitate or Innovate? Children's Innovation Is Influenced by the Efficacy of Observed Behavior," *Cognition* 142 (2015): 322–332.

25. N. Ratner and J. Bruner, "Games, Social Exchange and the Acquisition of Language," *Journal of Child Language* 5, no. 3 (1978): 391–401.

26. F. Subiaul, E. Krajkowski, E. E. Price, and A. Etz, "Imitation by Combination: Preschool Age Children Evidence Summative Imitation in a Novel Problem-Solving Task," *Frontiers in Psychology* 6 (2015), article 1410.

27. M. Nielsen, "Imitation, Pretend Play, and Childhood: Essential Elements in the Evolution of Human Culture," *Journal of Comparative Psychology* 126, no. 2 (2012): 170–181.

28. C. Sunstein and R. Thaler, "The Two Friends Who Changed How We Think about How We Think," review of *The Undoing Project: A Friendship That Changed Our Minds,* by Michael Lewis, *New Yorker,* December 7, 2016.

29. M. Lewis, *The Undoing Project: A Friendship That Changed Our Minds* (New York: W. W. Norton, 2016), 132.

30. M. Eddy, "This 14-Year-Old Prodigy Does Not Want to Be Called 'a New Mozart,'" *New York Times,* June 14, 2019, A8.

4. Ideas

Epigraph: Ursula, quoted in S. Isaacs, *Intellectual Growth in Young Children: With an Appendix on Children's "Why" Questions by Nathan Isaacs* (New York: Harcourt, Brace, 1931; repr. London: Routledge, 2018), 365.

1. P. Gay, *Freud: A Life for Our Time* (New York: W. W. Norton, 1998).

2. Galen, *Works on Human Nature: Volume 1, Mixtures (De Temperamentis),* trans. P. N. Singer and P. J. van der Eijk (Cambridge, UK: Cambridge University Press, 2018); Hippocrates, *Volume I: Ancient Medicine,* trans. W. H. S. Jones, Loeb Classical Library 147 (Cambridge, MA: Harvard University Press, 1923).

3. A. Abu-Asab, H. Amri, and M. S. Micozzi, *Avicenna's Medicine: A New Translation of the 11th-Century Canon with Practical Applications for Integrative Health Care* (New York: Simon and Schuster, 2013).

4. H. von Helmholtz, *Helmholtz's Treatise on Physiological Optics Volume III,* ed. J. P. C. Southall (Menasha, WI: Optical Society of America, 1925), 1866.

5. A. Shtulman and J. Valcarcel, "Scientific Knowledge Suppresses But Does Not Supplant Earlier Intuitions," *Cognition* 124, no. 2 (2012): 209–215; K. E. Stanovich and R. F. West, "Reasoning Independently of Prior Belief and Individual Differences in Actively Open-Minded Thinking," *Journal of Educational Psychology* 89, no. 2 (1997): 342–357; J. W. Stigler, K. B. Givvin, and B. J. Thompson, "What Community College Developmental Mathematics Students Understand about Mathematics," *MathAMATYC Educator* 1, no. 3 (2010): 4–16; D. Kuhn, *Education for Thinking* (Cambridge MA: Harvard University Press, 2008).

6. J. W. Astington, P. L. Harris, and D. R. Olson, eds., *Developing Theories of Mind* (Cambridge, UK: Cambridge University Press, 1988).

7. I borrow the term from literary theory. See, for example, T. Todorov, *Mikhail Bakhtin: The Dialogical Principle,* trans. Wlad Godzich (Manchester, UK: Manchester University Press, 1984).

8. Anna Deloi, "Storytellers and Philosophers: How Children Learn to Think about Ideas," Senior Honors Thesis, Williams College, 2018.

9. P. L. Harris, "Children's Understanding of Death: From Biology to Religion," *Philosophical Transactions of the Royal Society B: Biological Sciences* 373, no. 1754 (2018): 20170266.

10. M. Giménez and P. Harris, "Children's Acceptance of Conflicting Testimony: The Case of Death," *Journal of Cognition and Culture* 5, no. 1–2 (2005): 143–164.

11. W. Faulkner, *As I Lay Dying* (New York: Jonathan Cape and Harrison Smith, 1930).

12. P. Boero, N. Douek, and R. Garuti, "Children's Conceptions of Infinity of Numbers in a Fifth-Grade Classroom Discussion Context," paper presented at the 27th International Group for the Psychology of Mathematics Education Conference, Honolulu, July 2003, vol. 2, 121–128, https://files.eric.ed.gov/fulltext/ED500910.pdf, quotes 125.

13. I. Wistedt and M. Martinsson, "Orchestrating a Mathematical Theme: Eleven-Year-Olds Discuss the Problem of Infinity," *Learning and Instruction* 6, no. 2 (1996): 173–185, quote 179–180.

14. L. Kohlberg, *Essays on Moral Development,* vol. 1: *The Philosophy of Moral Development* (San Francisco: Harper and Row, 1981).

15. P. R. Blake and K. McAuliffe, "'I Had So Much It Didn't Seem Fair': Eight-Year-Olds Reject Two Forms of Inequity," *Cognition* 120, no. 2 (2011): 215–224. P. R. Blake, K. McAuliffe, and F. Warneken, "The Developmental Origins of Fairness: The Knowledge–Behavior Gap," *Trends in Cognitive Sciences* 18, no. 11 (2014): 559–561.

16. C. E. Smith, P. R. Blake, and P. L. Harris, "I Should but I Won't: Why Young Children Endorse Norms of Fair Sharing but Do Not Follow Them," *PLoS One* 8, no. 3 (2013): e59510.

17. C. C. Helwig and U. Jasiobedzka, "The Relation between Law and Morality: Children's Reasoning about Socially Beneficial and Unjust Laws," *Child Development* 72, no. 5 (2001): 1382–1393.

18. M. Schäfer, D. B. Haun, and M. Tomasello, "Fair Is Not Fair Everywhere," *Psychological Science* 26, no. 8 (2015): 1252–1260.

19. W. Damon, *Moral Child: Nurturing Children's Natural Moral Growth* (New York: Simon and Schuster, 2008), quote from 42–44.

20. J. Piaget, *The Child's Conception of the World,* trans. J. Tomlinson and A. Tomlinson (London: Kegan Paul, Trench, Trubner, 1929).

21. Piaget, *The Child's Conception of the World,* 202.

22. L. P. Butler and E. M. Markman, "Finding the Cause: Verbal Framing Helps Children Extract Causal Evidence Embedded in a Complex Scene," *Journal of Cognition and Development* 13, no. 1 (2012): 38–66.

23. N. Pramling, "'The Clouds Are Alive Because They Fly in the Air as If They Were Birds': A Re-Analysis of What Children Say and Mean in Clinical Interviews in the Work of Jean Piaget," *European Journal of Psychology of Education* 21, no. 4 (2006): 453–466.

24. G. B. Matthews, *Dialogues with Children* (Cambridge, MA: Harvard University Press, 1984).

25. K. Bartsch and H. M. Wellman, *Children Talk about the Mind* (New York: Oxford University Press, 1995), 40.

26. C. Baer and O. Friedman, "Fitting the Message to the Listener: Children Selectively Mention General and Specific Facts," *Child Development* 89, no. 2 (2018): 461–475.

27. I. Bascandziev and P. L. Harris, "The Role of Testimony in Young Children's Solution of a Gravity-Driven Invisible Displacement Task," *Cognitive Development* 25, no. 3 (2010): 233–246.

28. Deloi, "Storytellers and Philosophers."

29. C. A. Schult and H. M Wellman, "Explaining Human Movements and Actions: Children's Understanding of the Limits of Psychological Explanation," *Cognition* 62, no. 3 (1997), 291–324.

30. H. M. Wellman, A. K. Hickling, and C. A. Schult, "Young Children's Psychological, Physical, and Biological Explanations," in H. M. Wellman and K. Inagaki, eds., *The Emergence of Core Domains of Thought: New Directions for Child and Adolescent Development,* no. 75, New Directions for Child Development series (New York: Jossey-Bass, 1997): 7–25, quotes 21.

31. A. K. Hickling and H. M. Wellman, "The Emergence of Children's Causal Explanations and Theories: Evidence from Everyday Conversation," *Developmental Psychology* 37, no. 5 (2001): 668–683.

32. A. G. Greenwald, "The Totalitarian Ego: Fabrication and Revision of Personal History," *American Psychologist* 35, no. 7 (1980): 603–618.

33. M. R. Banaji and A. G. Greenwald, *Blindspot: Hidden Biases of Good People* (New York: Random House Delacorte, 2013), 34–41.

34. A. G. Greenwald and M. R. Banaji, "The Implicit Revolution: Reconceiving the Relation between Conscious and Unconscious," *American Psychologist* 72, no. 9 (2017): 861–871.

35. M. J. Sandstrom and R. Jordan, "Defensive Self-Esteem and Aggression in Childhood," *Journal of Research in Personality* 42, no. 2 (2008): 506–514.

36. Mark Hensch, "Clinton: We Must Fight 'Implicit Bias,'" *The Hill,* September 26, 2016.

37. L. Wright, *Remembering Satan* (New York: Knopf, 1994); J. Sherman, B. Gawronski, and Y. Trope, *Dual-Process Theories of the Social Mind* (New York: Guilford Press, 2014).

5. The Idea Workshop

Epigraph: E. Duckworth, *The Having of Wonderful Ideas and Other Essays on Teaching and Learning* (New York: Teachers College Press, 2006).

1. B. Hart and T. R. Risley, *Meaningful Differences in the Everyday Experience of Young American Children* (Baltimore, MD: Paul H Brookes Publishing, 1995).

2. J. Brooks-Gunn, A. S. Fuligni, and L. Berlin. *Early Child Development in the 21st Century: Profiles of Current Research Initiatives* (New York: Teachers College, 2003).

3. D. A. Phillips and J. P. Shonkoff, eds., *From Neurons to Neighborhoods: The Science of Early Childhood Development* (Washington, DC: National Academies Press, 2000); D. L. Kirp, *The Sandbox Investment: The Preschool Movement and Kids-First Politics* (Cambridge, MA: Harvard University Press, 2009); J. J. Heckman, *Giving Kids a Fair Chance* (Cambridge, MA: MIT Press, 2013).

4. D. Kelemen, "The Magic of Mechanism: Explanation-Based Instruction on Counterintuitive Concepts in Early Childhood," *Perspectives on Psychological Science* 14, no. 4 (2019): 510–522.; D. Kelemen, N. A. Emmons, R. Seston Schillaci, and P. A. Ganea, "Young Children Can Be Taught Basic Natural Selection Using a Picture-Storybook Intervention," *Psychological Science* 25, no. 4 (2014): 893–902; T. Ruffman, L. Slade, and E. Crowe, "The Relation between Children's and Mothers' Mental State Language and Theory-of-Mind Understanding," *Child Development* 73, no. 3 (2002): 734–751.

5. E. Bonawitz, correspondence with author, 2018.

6. Deborah Loewenberg Ball, "Mathematical Knowledge for Teaching," video, accessible at https://www.youtube.com/watch?v=leasL_kk8XM.

7. William Pene du Bois, *Lion* (New York: Viking Press, 1956).

8. C. E. Snow, "Academic Language and the Challenge of Reading for Learning about Science," *Science* 328, no. 5977 (2010): 450–452; C. E. Snow, P. Uccelli, and C. White, "The Conditions for and Significance of Children's Acquisition of Academic Language," unpublished manuscript; B. A. Fonseca and M. T. Chi, "Instruction Based on Self-Explanation," in *Handbook of Research on Learning and Instruction,* eds. R. E. Mayer and P. A. Alexander, 296–321 (New York: Routledge, 2011); J. Riley and D. Reedy, "Developing Young Children's Thinking through Learning to Write Argument," *Journal of Early Childhood Literacy* 5, no. 1 (2005): 29–51.

9. S. Sengupta, "Becoming Greta: 'Invisible Girl' to Global Climate Activist, with Bumps along the Way," *New York Times,* February 18, 2019.

Acknowledgments

Several friends and colleagues gave me invaluable help as I worked on this book. They offered new information, a fresh way to think about something, or just strong pushback. Some may not even have realized they were helping me. I thank Kathleen Corriveau, Kathy Erickson, Steve Fein, Howard Gardner, Paul Harris, Chris Moore, Leyla Rouhi, Jenno Topping, and the students in my seminar: Inquiry, Invention, and Ideas. A special thanks to Whitney Sandford for boundless energy in helping with various aspects of the project.

As always, I thank the many children, parents, and teachers who so graciously let me into their lives and their thoughts. I couldn't do what I do without them. A special word of appreciation for Roger Bolton, who first told me about his childhood more than twenty years ago. His riveting description stayed with me all these many years, and when I pleaded with him to tell me more, he did.

I thank Andrew Kinney, the editor who shepherded this project from its inception. He has the remarkable capacity to fully grasp what an author is trying to do, and yet make it better. In a world where there are so few editors of his caliber, I can't believe I get to work with him. I thank Julia Kirby, the attentive and meticulous editor who worked on the last draft of this book, and so improved the manuscript.

For providing me with endless conversations that help me think my thoughts, I thank Jake Levin, Silka Glanzman, Will Levin, Nicole Campanale, and Sam Levin.

A lot of bad things happened in the world while I was working on this book. But two amazingly wonderful things happened, as well: the births of my grandchildren, Henry Levin and Lina Levin. I dedicate this book to them.

Index

Index

Authoritative voice, 186
Avicenna, 113
Awe, arousing children's interest and, 60

Babies: detecting novelty in their environment, 16–19; differences between toddler and, 17–18; investigating new objects and events and reducing uncertainty, 17; investigatory repertoire, 17; sense of fairness and, 135–136
Background information, invention and, 83, 88
Baker, Ella, 140
Baker, Stacey, 25–26
Ball, Deborah, 182–184
Banaji, Mahsarin, 162, 163–164, 165
Bartsch, Karen, 150–152
Bascandziev, Igo, 152–153
Bath toys, child using pail as submarine, 69–71
The Beast in the Jungle (James), 13
Beck, Sarah, 79–81, 83, 98
Beery, Thomas, 33–34
Behavior: children's ideas about behavior guiding, 138–139; driven by unseen psychological forces, 113–114; inherited, 9; moral, 136
Belize, children's questions in, 28–29
Bell, Alex, 89–90
Berlyne, Daniel, 22
Biological understanding of death, 121
Black Like Me (Griffin), 133
Black students, underperformance of on intellectual ability tests, 9–10
Blake, Peter, 134–135, 136–137
Blickets, experiments featuring, 96, 144–145
Boero, Paolo, 128–129
Bolton, Roger, 64–67; childhood pursuits, 66–67, 106–107, 108; professional accomplishments, 64–66
Bonawitz, Elizabeth "Liz," 22–23, 60, 178–179, 201n12
Books, children who love, 50–52
Breuer, Josef, 112
Brown, Ann, 47–48
Bruner, Jerome, 47, 100

Bugzeeland / Bugzeelish, invention of, 77–79
Butler, Lucas, 144–145

Can-tabs project, 189–192; children's sculptures, 191–192; as means to explore subjectivity, 172–173
Carey, Susan, 33
Carr, K., 99
Categories, kinds unknowingly applied to matters requiring judgment, 162–163
Causal explanations, 24–25; exposure at early age to, 178
Causal hypotheses: conjunctive, 97–98; disjunctive, 97
Causal links, children differentiating good from bad, 23
Causal reasoning, 95–98
Causation: assembling framework for constructing theories of by age three, 161; children making abstract connections between cause and effect, 24; using stories to explain, 160–161
Causes, learning to identify, 95–98
Cave, children making a, 75–77
Character education, 176
Charcot, Jean-Marie, 112
Chetty, Raj, 89–90
Chi, Micheline, 39, 40–41
Child Language Data Exchange System (CHILDES), 55–56, 161
Children: adults' ignorance of child's intellectual lives, 8, 12; asking questions, 27–31; choosing which surprises to notice and pursue, 19; copycatting and, 98–101; difficulty in inventing on demand, 91–92; interest in natural world, 31–33; links between intellectual experiences of young children and academic successes of adolescents, 177; losing drive to concoct ideas as age, 10; morality and, 131–139; observing, 10–12; polyphonics and, 118; processes leading to formation of ideas, 5, 7; sensitivity to epistemological nature of exchanges, 144–145; stages of moral development, 134; urge to reduce

Index